Women's Soul Stories of
Remembering, Reclaiming & Rising

EMBERS to Wings

Compiled by Linda Joy
Edited by Deborah Kevin, Linda Dessau,
and Chelsea Seegmiller

A Sacred Gift to
Strengthen Your Heart & Nourish Your Inner World

Discover the power of soul-infused affirmations designed to remind you of your truth, wisdom, and feminine power as you rise into who you are becoming.

Your I RISE Manifesto & Affirmation Posters Gift Set Includes:

- The I RISE Manifesto Poster — *a powerful declaration to anchor you in remembrance, courage, and self-trust*

- An Affirmation Poster — *created to gently elevate your mindset and support you in embodying your inner strength and sacred feminine wisdom*

These beautiful printable posters are meant to be displayed as daily reminders that you are rising — from within — guided by your heart and your truth.

It's time to remember your power and honor the woman you are becoming.

Download your complimentary gift at:
www.InspiredLivingPublishing.com/rise-gift

ISBN: 979-8-9911626-3-0
ebook ISBN: 979-8-9911626-4-7
Library of Congress Control Number: Applied for

Published by Inspired Living Publishing, LLC.
P.O. Box 1149, Lakeville, MA 02347
(508) 265-7929

Cover and interior design: Lisa Hromada (www.LoveIsTheSeed.com)

Interior layout: Patricia Creedon (www.patcreedondesigns.com)

Managing Editor: Deborah Kevin, MA (www.deborahkevin.com)

Associate Editors: Linda Dessau (www.ldeditorial.com/), Chelsea Seegmiller

Linda Joy photo credit: Ali Rosa Photography (www.alirosaphotography.com/)

Dedication

This book is dedicated to:

> To every woman who has ever stood in the ashes—unsure, unseen, underestimated—and still felt something inside her whisper, not yet … you were meant for more.
>
> To the ones who rose slowly, quietly, without applause.
>
> To the ones who rose fiercely, flames still clinging to their heels.
>
> To the ones who are rising now, one trembling breath at a time.
>
> **This book is for you.**

And, also to:

Niki, my daughter, who inspires me daily with her loving and compassionate heart, and as the sacred role model for her own daughter, Makenna.

Makenna (a.k.a. "The Little Goddess"), my spirited, creative, love-filled fourteen-year-old granddaughter: May you always embrace your magic and magnificence, my love, and never dull your sparkle.

Tyler, my grandson: May you remember your truth and magic and find the greatest peace and happiness in that truth.

Dana, the love of my life: Thirty-two years in and you still rock my world and melt my heart.

To the authors of *Embers to Wings* who dove in wholeheartedly, despite their vulnerability, to share their stories of being forged in life's fires, transformed by alchemy, and called to rise. May their stories inspire and empower you to believe in your inner power.

The magical team of talented individuals with whom I have been honored, blessed, and humbled to work with to bring this soulful project to life: Deborah Kevin, chief editor on this sacred project, who brings the essence of each story to light, and Linda Dessau and Chelsea Seegmiller, associate editors, for holding loving space for their stories to be told.

Lisa Hromada for the stunning cover and interior design, Patricia Creedon for the interior content layout, and Kim Turcotte, my Goddess of Operations and soul sister, who organizes and brings my visions to life.

And finally, to:

> You, the reader—may these pages remind you that you were never broken—only becoming. That your rising is not a miracle reserved for others—it is your birthright.

> With reverence for your journey, your voice, and your light—this book is placed in your hands as a mirror, a lantern, and a promise:

> *You were never meant to stay in the ashes.*

Also by Inspired Living Publishing
Inspired Living Publishing's best-selling titles include:

Stress Relief Meditation Mandala Adult Coloring Book for Women: 33 Relaxing Designs with Energy-Infused Affirmations & a Powerful Stress Relief Meditation & Affirmation Gift Set by Lisa Hromada

The Art of Self-Nurturing: A Field Guide to Living with More Peace, Joy & Meaning by Kelley Grimes, MSW

Broken Open: Embracing Heartache and Betrayal as Gateways to Unconditional Love by Mal Duane

Soul-Hearted Living: A Year of Sacred Reflections & Affirmations for Women by Dr. Debra Reble

Everything Is Going to Be Okay!: From the Projects to Harvard to Freedom by Dr. Catherine Hayes, CPCC

Being Love: How Loving Yourself Creates Ripples of Transformation in Your Relationship and the World by Dr. Debra Reble

Awakening to Life: Your Sacred Guide to Consciously Creating a Life of Purpose, Magic, and Miracles by Patricia Young

The Art of Inspiration: An Editor's Guide to Writing Powerful, Effective Inspirational & Personal Development Books by Bryna Haynes.

As well as these best-selling titles in our sacred anthology division:

Divine Synchronicity: Women's Stories of Magic, Miracles & Manifesting

Life Shifts: Women's Stories of Surrendering to and Rising Above Life's Challenges

Reclaiming Your Midlife Mojo: Women's Stories of Self-Discovery & Transformation

Life Reimagined! Women's Stories of Hope, Resilience & Transformation

SHINE! Stories to Inspire You to Dream Big, Fear Less & Blaze Your Own Trail

Courageous Hearts: Soul-Nourishing Stories to Inspire You to Embrace Your Fears and Follow Your Dreams

Midlife Transformation: Redefining Life, Love, Health and Success

Inspiration for a Woman's Soul: Opening to Gratitude & Grace

Inspiration for a Woman's Soul: Cultivating Joy

Inspiration for a Woman's Soul: Choosing Happiness

Embracing Your Authentic Self: Women's Stories of Self-Discovery & Transformation

A Juicy, Joyful Life: Inspiration from Women Who Have Found the Sweetness in Every Day

Unleash Your Inner Magnificence (ebook only)

The Wisdom of Midlife Women 2 (ebook only)

You can find most of the titles at major online retailers and bookstores by request.

PRAISE FOR

EMBERS *to Wings*

For the women ready to rise! *Embers to Wings: Women's Soul Stories of Remembering, Reclaiming & Rising* is a soul-stirring anthology of true stories from courageous women who answered the quiet whisper: *It's time to rise.* Women who walked through fire and emerged, not as who they were before, but as who they were always meant to be. Their stories are testaments to the power of remembering who you are, reclaiming your voice, and rising with wings forged in flame. A must-read for all women!

CHRISTY WHITMAN
New York Times *bestselling author of*
The Art of Having It All

A powerful chorus of women telling their truth—sharing stories that don't just entertain, they awaken. It offers unapologetic permission to transform, release control, and trust the Divine. With reflection questions that spark profound change, you'll see where you've dimmed your light and how to rise, even when it's terrifying.

DR. ELLEN ALBERTSON
The Midlife Whisperer®

Embers to Wings: Women's Soul Stories of Remembering, Reclaiming &
Rising helps us remember our truth, reclaim our feminine power,
and helps raise the world's vibration.

AMY LEIGH MERCREE

World-renowned medical intuitive and bestselling author of nineteen
books and decks, including The Healing Home and The Atomic Element
Healing Oracle

Embers to Wings is a call to every woman's heart to remember we
can rise. The stories aren't the result of ease, but rather evidence
of life-defining choices that women have made with both courage
and faith in themselves and in something more. Let this book be
your spark to listen to your fire within!

LYNDA MONK, MSW, RSW, CPCC

Director of the International Association
for Journal Writing

Through vulnerable, heartfelt stories, *Embers to Wings* reflects the
shared human experience of rising above circumstances that attempt to dim our light. Each story is a testament to the human
spirit's ability to rise above the painful experiences we encounter
on our journey and shine again.

DAWN MICHELE JACKSON

Grief recovery method specialist and bestselling author of Journey to
Peace and Healing *and* Journey to Self-Discovery

Along our journey from the ashes of our personal experiences. Through the agreement to allow the embers to always sparkle and patiently wait within us to ignite and become the fire of our truth, guiding us to spread our wings, we all encounter human challenges and moments of choice to become. This collection of vulnerable, true-life stories, compiled by Linda Joy and edited by Deborah Kevin, is a guiding light on the path. Reading the stories opened my heart. Journaling on the reflective questions that followed each story was an invitation to another layer of healing. Read every story at least twice. Read between the lines and take the gifts these stories offer into your journey, your life. We are all meant to spread our wings, soar, and fly.

EFRAT SHOKEF, PHD

author of award-winning books: The Promise We Made *and*
UniverSoul Promises

Embers to Wings is a tender and powerful reminder that rising up almost always begins in the ashes. Through raw vulnerability and sacred honesty, the women in this book give us permission to trust the ember within and know that our transformation is forged in the fire. This book is your invitation to trust the flame within, to honor the dark night of the soul as sacred initiation, and to remember that no matter what trials you may face, you are not broken; you are becoming.

SHANN VANDER LEEK
Transformation goddess and podcast whisperer

Foreword

LISA MICHAELS

$\mathcal{N}$ow more than ever, women are feeling the call to shed the stories, beliefs, and conditioning they have carried for years, the ones that kept them feeling less than, unheard, or quietly shamed. This calling is no accident. We are being invited to remember our truth, reclaim our feminine power, and, in our own beautiful and unique ways, make a meaningful difference in our lives, our families, and our communities. Women are ready to fully own that they are worthy of living in their authentic essence, not someday, but now.

For nearly three decades, I have held sacred space for women's stories, their heartbreak, their awakening, and the reclamation of their soul gifts as they rise beyond cultural conditioning, distorted beliefs about themselves, and disconnection from the natural world and their own inner knowing. My own life reflects this profound feminine reclamation journey as well, as I have navigated loss, initiation, remembering, and ultimately, coming home to my deeper truth and purpose.

Again and again, I have witnessed women who, despite outer success in career and life, feel emotionally drained, burned out, and disconnected from themselves, even empty and frustrated from endless doing and producing. These women fiercely crave nourishment, rest, creativity, and deeper meaning, even if they don't yet have language for their longing for feminine ways of being.

Each woman wants to strengthen her self-esteem, trust herself more deeply, and reclaim her confident, embodied feminine voice and leadership. And as she does, she begins to seek new ways of living and leading, ways that honor the rhythms of the natural world, support the earth and future generations, and restore her vitality. She is drawn to new models of cooperation, collaboration, growth, guidance, and sustainable success, rooted in relationship, integrity, and soul-aligned purpose rather than sacrifice and depletion.

She longs to use her intuition, emotional intelligence, and relational gifts in life and business as naturally as she uses her intellect. She desires prosperity and success, yes—and she also yearns to live in right relationship with nature, with others, and with her own soul. She wants her passion, purpose, and prosperity to be replenished in ways that feel life-giving and true. And she is ready to remember her innate power of creation and her authentic feminine leadership.

Publisher & Authentic Storytelling® guide Linda Joy exemplifies a woman who has listened intensely to her soul's calling through life's painful initiations and risen with courage to spread her leadership wings. For years, she has shown women new ways to collaborate, reclaim visibility, and courageously share the depth of their stories in service to healing and collective awakening.

For nearly two decades, I have witnessed Linda's unwavering devotion and the extraordinary women drawn to her community. She leads with intuitive wisdom, heartfelt presence, and authentic service, creating sacred spaces where each woman is supported in embracing the truth of who she is and who she is becoming.

The journey from the embers of the soul's transformational fires to the emergence of your wings is not without perilous moments. Especially in times of grief, change, or uncertainty, it is easy to become entangled in false beliefs about yourself. The voices that whisper, *I'm not enough, I don't belong, I can't trust anyone, not even myself,* can tighten their grip when you are most vulnerable.

Sometimes all that is needed is a single flicker of light, a compassionate voice, a sacred story that meets you in the darkness and reminds you that you are not alone, and you are not lost. Someone who reflects that you are in the depths of transformation, not at the end of your road, and that you are meant to keep going.

The sacred stories in this book offer precisely that. They shine a light through the shadows. This book becomes a beacon of trust and inner knowing, reminding you that you will make it through and that you are being guided back to the wellspring of wisdom that has always lived within your soul.

As you receive these precious words and the courage woven through them, may you feel the quiet strength and deep remembrance they carry. May they gently guide you back to your own truth, your own wisdom, and the wings that have always been waiting to open.

With love and reverence for your journey,
Lisa Michaels
Nature-aligned life and soul prosperity mentor and author
Lisa-Michaels.com

Table of Contents

Wings Remembered: Integration

Introduction

LINDA JOY

There is a moment in every woman's life—not loud, not celebrated, not even visible to the outside world—when she realizes she cannot stay where she is. Her body may still be trembling. Her heart may still be broken. Her life may still be smoldering around her. Yet something inside her flickers.

A knowing.
A whisper.
An ember.

I know this moment intimately. I have lived it more than once.

There were years of my life when rising felt impossible. Years when the image I had of myself was shaped not by my soul, but by circumstances—circumstances that told me I wasn't enough, didn't belong, and would never become the woman I secretly dreamed of being.

I didn't grow up imagining myself as a mindset elevation coach, best-selling publisher, spiritual entrepreneur, creatrix of inspirational women's events, or the curator of women's stories.

I grew up learning how to survive. And for a long time, I believed that survival was all I could hope for.

I was about twenty-three on a sweltering hot summer day when I found myself standing at the checkout counter of my local grocery store, clutching food stamps, praying the woman behind me wouldn't notice. I remember the weight of that moment so vividly: the buzzing fluorescent lights, the hum of the conveyor belt, the heat of shame burning behind my eyes.

My daughter, now forty-one, was just eighteen months old at the time. I was a single mother, terrified and exhausted, with no roadmap and no one telling me I could rise. I remember avoiding eye contact, holding my breath, and convincing myself that this—*this small, scared version of me*—was all I was allowed to be. But beneath the fear, beneath the labels, beneath the evidence of lack and limitation, something else was there.

A whisper from my soul.

That whisper didn't change my circumstances overnight, but it began to transform me. I didn't rise in a single moment. I rose in fragments—one decision, one truth, one terrifying step at a time. It wasn't a straight line. It wasn't pretty. But it was holy.

Every time I thought I was breaking, I was actually breaking open. Every time I thought I was failing, I was being forged. Every time the world told me I was too late, too much, or not enough, something wiser inside me said: *Rise anyway.*

Alchemy is not an abstract concept for me. It is the lived process of turning my pain into my purpose, my doubt into devotion, my wounds into wings. I didn't become who I am *in spite* of my ashes—I became who I am *because of* them.

Women often think they need clarity before they rise. They wait until they feel ready, healed, confident, or unafraid. But rising does not begin with certainty. Rising begins with unrest—an ache in the soul that whispers, *This is not where your story ends.*

Every woman in this book has felt that ache.

Every story you will read began with a moment that tried to break her. Some faced illness. Some endured betrayal. Some carried generational wounds or secrets so heavy they could barely breathe. Some were silenced by others; others silenced themselves.

And still … they rose. Not perfectly. Not painlessly. But powerfully.

Some rose slowly, their wings unfolding one quiver at a time. Others rose in a blaze, choosing themselves in a single, life-altering breath. Each rise is unique. Each rise is valid.

Each rise is sacred.

Embers to Wings is not a collection of breaking points; it is a gathering of women who chose to rise.

I believe women don't need more examples of perfection. They need evidence of what's possible—evidence that their pain has purpose, that their voice has power, and that their rising is not a miracle reserved for the lucky few, but a birthright encoded in their bones.

That is why these stories matter: These women did not wait to be saved; they became their own rescuers. They answered their own calls. Their stories offer not just inspiration, but *permission*—

Permission to rest. Permission to speak. Permission to burn down what no longer fits. Permission to rise without apology.

As you read, may something within you stir—an old knowing, a buried truth, the memory of your wings.

If you are here, if these words are in your hands, there is a reason. You may not know what it is yet, but something inside you does. Perhaps you're still in your ashes. Perhaps you're somewhere in the middle, wings half-formed, unsure if you're strong enough to fly.

Beautiful soul, let me tell you what no one told me in that grocery store line:

> *You are not broken.*
> *You are becoming.*
>
> *Your story does not end in the fire.*
> *It begins there.*

Your wings are not missing.
They are remembering.

Your rising is not a question.
It is a promise.

This book is that promise made visible.

Welcome to *Embers to Wings*. Your flight starts here.

To Your Rising,

Linda Joy
Publisher

When the Fire Comes

The moment everything falls apart.

There is a moment every woman on the path of becoming knows—the moment when life no longer holds together the way it once did. The fire arrives unannounced, burning through the familiar: a relationship ends, a diagnosis shatters certainty, a career collapses, a dream dissolves. I have stood in that fire more than once—on my knees, stripped of identity, certainty, and control in life and in business—wondering how everything I created could disappear so quickly.

These soul stories live in that sacred unraveling. They are not tales of failure, but of initiation. When the fire comes, it cracks us open and reveals what was never meant to last—and what cannot be destroyed. This chapter honors the moment before the rise, when ashes still smolder, and the first embers of transformation begin to glow.

Into the Light

RINAT DE PICCIOTTO

I've often reviewed the events of that February day in my mind: my mom and I walking the short path to the hospital, a bitter wind pushing us forward, as she drags her unhealed leg one painful step at a time. Both of us in relative silence, engulfed in the fear of what comes next.

This wasn't our first visit to the ER. It was one of many that followed another day inscribed in my memory—the day of the accident. A split second when cold, hard metal hit living flesh and bone, causing irreversible damage and repercussions that are still deeply felt in our lives. This was the day everything was thrown into chaos. It was the last day my father was alive, the last day my mom had full mobility and a living partner, the last day of my life as I knew it. Everything following that day was reorganized. First around my mother and her many needs, and only much later around mine.

My mom's multiple and severe injuries required years of medical care and follow-ups, surgeries, and rehabilitation, at the end of which she was still left with little function and a deeply questioning heart. The many visits and stays at the hospital, the constant medical checkups, the effort required to get through one obstacle only to be met by yet another left both of our spirits weary of the ongoing attempt at living, at creating a stable environment in which we could heal.

Somewhere between the third and fourth surgery, a veil of thick darkness descended over us. The emergency operation, the growing financial stress, the complete lack of justice the system was supposed to deliver, and straining family relationships created so much pressure, eventually breaking the tether from my mom's mind to this reality.

I saw it happening in slow motion—her mind, once vibrant and sharp, became dull and dark. As her body became frail, her mind was overcome by terrifying conspiracies. She feared everything and everyone, found threats in moving shadows, distrusted her companions and loved ones, and could barely get any sleep. For several weeks, I climbed into her bed at night, holding her as if she were a young child. It felt in those moments I was also holding myself. In my embrace, I was soothing both of our souls, seeking and pulling glimmers of light from beyond and infusing them back into our being.

In those days of darkness, as my mom was questioning the utility of her life, I was questioning the purpose of mine. The chaos created by the accident meant that I needed to step away from my job and career so I could focus on caregiving and still have a semblance of a life. With all my efforts poured into taking care of my mom's needs, mine seemed to be on hold temporarily. My singular focus at the beginning was to carry my mom through this challenging period, and I was blind to how I was neglecting myself, my emotions, and my needs. I found myself under a cloak of forgetfulness of who I was, and it was only through creating an intentional creative space that I began to remember that I, too, was grieving.

I was grieving the loss of my dad. I was grieving the loss of my mom as a vibrant and highly capable person, and I was grieving the loss of my career—along with my identity as a productive, mission-driven person. All the parts of me that I knew seemed to be lost. My pillars of strength and support, my sense of stability, and with it any idea of a future direction. It seemed in those days that both my mom and I were descending a black spiral staircase, feeling our way in the dark, not knowing where it would lead us, if anywhere at all.

That cold February day, when we found ourselves once again in the hospital, was the bottom of that dark staircase. The emergency room was so full that night that we needed to wait many hours to be seen. I held my mom's hand in an effort to comfort her even as I myself was seeking comfort. It wasn't until the following day that a psychiatrist came by to run his assessment. His questions, innocuous as they were, seemed prosecutorial: Where was she born? When did she marry? How many children did she have? How long has she been widowed …?

My mom could gather just enough words to make out a reply, her mind struggling to remain in the conversation. And then … what did she do for a living? I could see my mom's face become even more distorted, shame overtaking her ability to talk.

"I … I … I …." The unspoken sentence hung heavily in the air.

Hot tears came flowing down my face. I couldn't bear her pain or mine. Pain of missed opportunities, pain of unacknowledged desires. Pain of dreams still locked inside. I didn't know where her shame ended and mine began, only the burning sensation of unfulfillment and a sense of longing so deep that it felt like a punch in the gut.

The following days were a blur—more assessments, medication changes, tests, bargaining with my mom to eat, and with her soul to stay in this world longer. I could feel her slipping away as she forgot how to walk and go to the bathroom. But even as her physical, mental, and emotional bodies were deteriorating, I could see a flicker of the light within.

I called it forth.

"I need you," I said. "I'm not ready for you to leave yet." And in my heart, I felt the ache of all the possibilities we hadn't explored yet, the life experiences that were still awaiting us, the promise of gentler mornings, of deeply held yearnings manifesting, of soul expressions that pierce through the darkness. In the ache of the possibility of non-being, I felt a pull toward the most profound expression of living from the center of who I was. From the grain of truth, the seed of creation that put us here to be all that we can be.

In that hospital room, as I pleaded, we began ascending the spiral back into the light.

We moved through the next few days with caution. Every hour both an agony and a blessing. Hours turned into days and days into weeks. A slow persistence of living seemed to push us forward. It came through the soul whispers to ground in nature, to look up at the sun and bathe in its rays, to spend spring days in the garden—taking in all the magnificent details of creation. To allow hope and life to retake root.

It came through in the whispers to once again step into service, not from a place of self-abandonment, but from a place of desire. It came through the invitation to claim my power as a creator—to pour my life force into my own creativity and expression, to open myself up to people and opportunities, to see myself as profoundly held by those I have shared my life with and by Life itself. It came through in the quiet knowing that there is a deeper mission and calling that I must step into, in creating an intentional practice to hold my own becoming as I hold others'.

Spring days turned to summer, and with it, bolder action. The more I delved into myself, the more I could acknowledge my value, the more I could allow myself to receive others' appreciation, support, and encouragement. The more I gave from my center, the more I received in return. Not the offering of sacrifice, but the giving of a whole heart ready to share its soul song.

The spark of life I felt at the bottom of the spiral staircase was the spark of a reawakening to my truth, to the preciousness of life, and to the knowledge that we are here for a reason—a mission instilled in our soul and embedded as a blueprint for our being, here, at this time. A blueprint we all carry, which, when tuned into, can show us our way back into the light.

Reflection

1. When have you found light in the deepest darkness—
and how did that moment reshape your understanding of
yourself and your purpose?

2. In what ways have you learned to give from wholeness
rather than self-abandonment?

3. What inner truth or "soul whisper" continues to guide
you as you rise into the woman you are becoming?

A Shimmer of Light

SHARIE HOHN

One day, in despair, I told my mother I was done. I was ready to end it all. Her response stunned me: "Come get me, because I'm going with you." Her words jolted me. Something shifted. I sat at the window, staring at the trees outside, and whispered: *Sharie, you've done this for others, you can do this for yourself too.* I rose from the couch, made a nourishing meal, took some herbs for my nervous system and stepped outside to touch the tree I had been staring at. That was the first step back.

I wasn't the typical girl who dreamed of motherhood. From an early age, I was drawn to something different. At twelve, I felt the spark of independence, the vision of freedom, travel, and a business of my own. I had a role model who embodied those possibilities: my mother's best friend. She showed me a woman could live on her own terms, and on my twenty-sixth birthday, I signed the papers to purchase my first health food store. It wasn't a coincidence—I had been following the threads of energy guiding me all along.

That path began earlier than I realized. At fourteen, I faced a health crisis that doctors dismissed with little more than broth and crackers. My mother, unwilling to accept that answer, took me to a homeopath. Within three days, I was well. That experience altered the course of my life. It opened me up to new ways of healing, questioning the prescribed path, and exploring spirituality in ways that felt more authentic than what I had been taught.

Through my teens and into college, I immersed myself in health and alternative approaches. While attending business school, I worked at a local health food store, where I learned not only about supplements but also about people. From there, I moved into management and, eventually, ownership.

The store flourished. Out of more than fifty in the franchise, it became the most successful, reaching over a million dollars in annual sales. Yet the true measure of success wasn't numbers—it was in the faces of the people who came with their worries and questions. It was in the conversations we shared, in the way they trusted me with their stories. Looking into their eyes, I could see the deeper patterns of what had brought them there. It was never just about selling products; it was about soul-level connection.

With that rise came tension. At home, my growing success wasn't always celebrated by the man in my life at the time. Comments surfaced that I was rising too high, that I risked appearing egotistical. At the same time, I was pushed to make more, to keep producing. The contradiction wore on me: Don't shine too brightly, but don't stop striving. I tried to dim myself to avoid conflict, but each time I hid, something inside me withered.

Still, my vision expanded. I saw ways to grow beyond supplements into supporting whole lifestyles of health and empowerment. But whenever I shared these ideas, doors closed. My proposals met resistance. It began to feel like chains were fastening tighter with every attempt to move forward. Beneath it all, financial pressures grew heavy and started to pull me under. I had learned early to be the strong one through my parents' separation when I was eleven. I took on the role of holding everything together, guiding others through turmoil and shutting down my own needs. My mother said that I had "steeled" myself as to not add any burden to them.

That pattern followed me into adulthood. I tried to save both my relationship and my business, even as they pulled me in opposite directions. Neither seemed to recognize my vision, and the weight grew unbearable. I lived in constant fear of losing everything—and then I did.

My relationship ended. The loss cut deep, not only of the relationship itself but the dream of what I thought it could be. I tried to move forward, but the business chains grew heavier. Rising costs, franchise fees, and rent made breathing feel impossible. And then another wound surfaced: the realization that I needed to heal my relationship with my father. A month later he suffered a stroke.

The moment I walked into the hospital and saw him lying there was a gut punch like no other. For the first time in my life, I lost control. I dropped to the floor, sobbing with a force I couldn't stop, while my mother watched in shock. I had always been the one who held it all together. But this moment shattered that image, and she had to drag me from the room. Eventually, I gathered myself enough to sit with him, to say I loved him and more but inside, I felt numb.

For weeks, I drove five hours back and forth, juggling the business with desperate visits to his side. Each time I arrived, more of him had slipped away. Until one morning, as I prepared to make the drive again, the call came. He was gone. Another whirlwind began—writing the eulogy, planning the service, managing a vacation I had booked. I made the five-hour trip once more, drove home the same day with his ashes, and the next morning boarded a plane. Sitting on a balcony in Mexico, staring at the ocean, I whispered: *What just happened to my life?* When I returned, my body gave out. For three months, I couldn't work. I tried to push on, to keep the business running, to train staff, to force myself back to function. But the cracks were too deep. I collapsed under the weight of it all. In that collapse, a doorway opened: the beginning of my true journey to health.

Recovery wasn't quick. The 2009 crash hit hard. The business couldn't survive, and bankruptcy followed just before my fortieth birthday. In searching for help, I chose a woman's name from the Yellow Pages to help me figure out a financial solution, determined to avoid old patterns. By chance, the name belonged to a man, yet he became the one who guided me through the loss. In time, I recognized the full measure of what I had lost: my relationship, my father, and now the business I had poured my life into. Every anchor I leaned on was gone. In that emptiness, I realized I no longer knew who I was.

That void became the beginning of transformation. I turned inward, deeper than ever before. I explored meditation, energy work, sound healing, chakra alignment, and ancestral practices. I spoke with my higher self, channeled guidance, and slowly began to knit my body, mind, and spirit back together. Healing touched not only my traumas and beliefs, but also my physical pain. When fear resurfaced in relationships, I chose freedom again, letting go of what would have dimmed me.

My beloved stepfather had become the support I yearned for from my own father. Later, as his health declined, new layers of his character revealed themselves. Pain burned down my left side—hip, leg, thigh—tied to the feminine line. As I listened deeper, I realized the truth: For generations, the women in my family had never been supported by men. That legacy lived in my body. No physical treatment reached it. Only through ancestral work did the energy shift, and my body began to heal. The pain became a teacher, guiding me to transcend not just my own wounds, but the unhealed weight of those who came before me.

The years have circled me back to the beginning. They've stripped me down through loss after loss, until only truth was left. They've forced me to discover my worth—not in roles, relationships, or achievements—but in who I am at my core. I trace it back to when I was eleven, when my father brought another family into our home after the breakup. In that moment, I lost my home, my place, and the father I adored. As an only child and daddy's girl, it was devastating. From then on, it seemed everything had to burn before I could rise again, proving my strength and resilience.

Now, I see it differently. I'm not starting over anymore. I am stepping into who I truly am: authentic, aligned, and free. What I've lived, learned, and healed has shown me this: Our worth is not in holding it all together for others, it's in how deeply we honor the truth of our being. The child who lost her place has become a woman who can relate through many experiences, who creates space for others to find theirs, not only at the human level, but also at the soul level.

This is where I shine.

Reflection

1. When have you mistaken strength for self-sacrifice—
and what shifted when you finally allowed yourself to
receive support?

2. What patterns or stories have you inherited from your
family line that you're ready to release or transform?

3. How has loss or collapse invited you to rediscover
who you truly are beneath roles, relationships, and
achievements?

Along Came a Spider

JENNIFER SULLIVAN

The weather in Northern California was perfect that first week of December as I stood with fifteen other men and women gathered from all over the world to study under three Grand Master Firewalk Facilitators and obtain a Master Firewalk Facilitator certification. The first fire of the week was lit, and we all watched it blaze as the flames rose over ten feet high, the embers carrying our intentions and prayers of the week up to the stars and heavens above.

I stood off to the side, thoroughly exhausted, in awe of how I was even there. I had been planning this adventure for almost a year, making payments, booking the flight, telling everyone how excited I was to continue my firewalking journey and bring back techniques to share with the community. But I almost didn't make it to this training … not due to flight delays, or normal travel "disasters," but due to a spider.

Only a few days earlier, I'd been lying in a hospital room, where I'd already been for several days. One of the nurses came to check on me, and she was concerned at the redness on my chest and that my breathing had changed. Having a history of anaphylaxis with medications, I had developed an allergic reaction to one of the new medications—the one that was currently hooked up, pumping its way into me. The rest of that night was a blur, but I remember a few things: The room was full of people, and I recall thinking to myself, "*Oh, this is a checkout point ... but I want to stay.*" The *Loxosceles reclusa*, more commonly known as the brown recluse spider, is less than half an inch, but it is a venomous little foe. These spiders can bite, and when they do, their venom can create a necrotic, tissue-rotting lesion. Around fourteen days before flying to California, I woke up with an itch on my lower back. Initially, I thought it might be a tick, and the location was one I couldn't easily see, no matter how creative I got with the positions of myself and mirrors in my bathroom. I went walking with a friend and had him look at it, and he said, "Well, you definitely got bit by something."

Immediately, I got the intuitive hit that it was a spider bite, but I wasn't overly concerned. Having grown up on a farm and living in cranberry bog country, wolf spiders are everywhere. They are harmless but can be intimidating. They rarely bite, and if they do, it isn't really anything to be concerned about. There might be some swelling or slight pain, but nothing overly dramatic. But because I had this training coming up, I decided to go to the doctor.

When the nurse practitioner said, "I want to get two of the doctors to look at this," I knew something was up. My physician, also a longtime family friend, came in and looked at it, and sighed. He explained it was a brown recluse bite. There had been a recent outbreak in the state of Massachusetts and there had been many people coming in with bites from these tiny creatures.

I was shocked. Where had it come from? Walking in the woods? Was it hiding in my winter sweaters or coats? And how do you even treat a bite by one of these things?

My doctor created a plan, stating he was going to do his best to keep me out of the hospital. I took oral and injectable antibiotics daily, and the tissue did not look necrotic, so we thought we had dodged a major bullet.

The fourth morning, I woke up at six thirty and knew immediately that things had taken a turn for the worse. I was drenched in sweat, dizzy, and vomiting. I managed to catch a glimpse in the mirror, where my fears were now confirmed: What had been a tiny little red mark was the size of a grapefruit, red and purple. I stumbled around, gathering what I would need, as I knew I would be admitted to the hospital, and dialed 911.

The paramedics arrived and helped me into the ambulance. They rolled their eyes when I told them it was a brown recluse bite, but when I lifted my shirt, they both let out a "Holy shit!" in shock, which solidified in my fever-addled mind that this was really bad.

After spending a lovely day in the emergency room, waiting for a bed, I was admitted. I was on twenty-four IV antibiotics, bags being changed every few hours, but I was determined to get better as quickly as possible. What kept me going was talking excitedly to my nurses and doctors about firewalking, showing them pictures and videos. Some were intrigued, while others kiddingly said I was crazy.

While the medical team did their part, my friends and spiritual community had stepped up, sending healing and protection, calling, texting, and visiting me, as well as taking care of my house and my two very confused cats. The facilitators of the firewalk training were in touch daily, hoping I would be able to make it, even though it seemed increasingly less likely. I was grateful that the tissue had not gone necrotic, but I was growing impatient with the infection's slow receding. I was restless and in limbo, having zero control over anything. I told my spirit team that this was ridiculous, and I wanted out.

The day after my anaphylactic reaction, I canceled my flight, calling off the training and releasing whatever little control I had. And that's when the magic happened—the following day, a new doctor was assigned to my case, one who had actually firewalked before. He said he understood that I had a training to go to, that firewalking was about empowerment, and that those who facilitate it have a calling. He said he would do everything in his power to get me to that training. Dr. Draggon (yes, that was his name) got the right combination of antibiotics going, and within forty-eight hours, I was released, with additional oral antibiotics to continue.

I called my mom to tell her I was rebooking the trip to California. I asked my friends if they would continue to watch the house and care for the cats, and they agreed, happy to support me since they knew I had been waiting for this. The fire called, and I answered. I got home, slept for half a day, threw clothes in a bag, and hopped on a plane.

I was welcomed and greeted by fourteen people I didn't know, all excited to be together and that I'd made it. Ryan, my dear friend whom I met during my first firewalk training, surprised me by also signing up for the mastery training. We both burst into tears when we saw each other. I couldn't believe that I would be able to complete a second training alongside Ryan and knew that I was exactly where I needed to be. There was even another participant who had also nearly died from a brown recluse bite, and we bonded over that.

That first night, the fire we built was in the shape of a dragon— giving it a face, tail, legs, and spines out of wood before igniting it. I laughed when we built it and offered a prayer of gratitude to Dr. Draggon, fellow firewalker. That night, we all watched the fire in awe, dancing around it and over the coals once they were spread, excited for the week of training to come, what we would learn, and how we would grow, bond, and step into the next evolution of ourselves.

I often say that walking across the coals isn't the challenge of firewalking. Getting to the actual firewalk is the hardest part. The commitment to yourself and your healing, letting go of the control we all desire to have throughout our day-to-day lives. That all disappears at a firewalk. It becomes about you stepping into your best and highest self—learning you are more capable than you realize, and you have walked through every fire you've come across in your life and come out on the other side.

The spirit of the fire has been my greatest teacher, because I allow it to be.

Reflection

1. What "fire" have you walked through in your own life? Think of a time when circumstances tested your strength or faith. What did you learn about yourself on the other side of that experience?

2. When have you had to surrender control to something greater? Describe a moment when you let go and allowed life—or Spirit—to guide you. How did that surrender shift what happened next?

3. What helps you trust that you're exactly where you need to be? How do you recognize guidance, support, or synchronicity when it appears? What reminds you to stay open to the "magic" in the unexpected?

The Perfect Life

NANCY OKEEFE

I grew up in the perfect home, in the perfect neighborhood, with the perfect family. It was a neighborhood of 1950s track homes in the suburbs. Five streets of nearly identical three-bedroom, one-bathroom ranch houses, each with a backyard for playing with the many children around the same age who lived there.

My parents were like the parents in a 1950s or 1960s sitcom—*The Adventures of Ozzie and Harriet*, *Leave it to Beaver*, or *Father Knows Best*. I don't remember them ever fighting. Dad went to work every day in the city; Mom managed the household. He did the repairs and built things for our home on the weekends. She cooked, baked, and sewed clothes for us, making sure we were all well cared for and felt loved. Almost every year, we took vacations, either to the beach or to another state. We laughed. We were encouraged. We were believed in. They made a wonderful life for my sister and me, and were happily married for sixty-seven years. That was the life model I was given. But no matter how hard I tried to recreate it, life had other ideas.

I married my high school sweetheart at eighteen, just after graduation. Soon, I learned I was expecting. My life was beginning, and I pictured a happy family in our own home with the man I loved. We laughed a lot. We were best friends. We never fought. He went to work every morning; I prepared our home for our new addition. I cooked dinner every evening and waited anxiously for him to come home so we could share our day and spend a loving evening together.

One Thursday evening, with a freshly roasted chicken on the table, he didn't come home. That morning, when he kissed me goodbye and backed out of the driveway, I never dreamed it would be the last time I ever saw him. He left me and never looked back. He didn't show up when our son was born. He didn't show up to court for the divorce. I had my beautiful baby boy alone. My dreams were crushed.

I went to work to support us while my mother graciously cared for my son during the day. For the next few years, I went through the motions of life—putting on a smile, hiding my sadness from my son, just trying to get by.

Then something miraculous happened. I changed jobs for a slightly larger paycheck and met a wonderful man. At twenty, with a child, it wasn't easy to meet someone, but he was different.

Ten years older and never married, he loved me—and he loved my son too. He adopted my son as his own. We bought a house. He went to work every day and came home every evening. We laughed. We were best friends. We never fought. We spent weekends together as a family, surrounded by his large, loving family, who accepted us with open arms. I felt certain I was back on the right path, and every day he confirmed it by the way he loved me.

We had a daughter together. Finally, I had the perfect family I had dreamed of. Life was perfect for eighteen years—until one cold December morning, just after breakfast, he died suddenly of a massive heart attack. I was thirty-eight.

I sank into a deep depression. I could barely function. I went through the motions, but the hole inside my heart was deep and unbearable. What was wrong with me that I couldn't have the life I wanted?

For my children, I forced myself to keep moving. They were reeling from their father's sudden death. My son had just started college, and I was determined to keep him there. He came home most weekends, and the three of us spent time together recounting our memories, trying to keep him alive in our hearts.

I couldn't cry. I bottled everything up. I smiled for the kids, told stories, and repeated his jokes. He had certain sayings, and I repeated them to the kids whenever I could. "It will make you a better person, and you could use it," he'd tease when the kids complained about doing their chores. I worked hard to make our life seem normal.

My son finished college and started a great job. My daughter finished her education and met the love of her life. They were thriving, and I felt proud. They had crossed the finish line. I was an empty nester now, roaming around in a quiet house with just my memories, feeling totally spent.

Then it hit me—my grief. Just when I thought I had conquered the worst, I realized I had never dealt with my own loss. It hit me like a wrecking ball.

I poured myself into work. I went back to school for my master's degree. I started my own company and grew it into a multimillion-dollar enterprise with employees in four states. I grew as a person. I processed my grief though action. On commutes, I worked through feelings to songs on the radio. On the weekends, I talked to my husband as if he were still there. I knew he was listening, because after those conversations, new ideas would pop into my thoughts.

One day, in one of our talks, I told him I was tired of being alone. It had been thirteen years since his death. I hadn't dated, only worked. Within days I met someone at a neighborhood social club my husband and I had once frequented. I know my husband sent him to me. This man knew my husband, though I had never met him. We dated. We fell in love. We moved in together. He was fun, a wonderful addition to my life. He shared his memories of my husband and let me process mine. With gentle love, he helped me heal my broken heart.

We've been together for twenty-one years, never married but deeply committed. In recent years, he has developed dementia. He doesn't remember yesterday's conversations, our vacations, anniversaries, birthdays, or holidays. He is leaving me too. This loss is slow and painful for both of us. His memories are gone, but we make new ones every day. I still see love in his eyes, and I feel honored by the trust he has placed in me to help him through this difficult part of his life.

I will never have a sixty-seven-year marriage. The clock has run out on that dream. But I have something I believe is even better. I have been loved deeply by three men, and I am thankful for each of them. We had wonderful times, and we had tragic times. It all burned down, more than once. But through it all, I kept my loving heart, my positive attitude, my faith in myself, and my ability to rise from the ashes of each relationship—stronger and better for having lived it.

Reflection

1. How has life invited you to release an ideal of "perfection" and embrace the beauty of what is real?

2. When have love and loss taught you more about your own strength than success or stability ever could?

3. What does "a perfect life" mean to you now, after all that you've experienced and overcome?

In the Ashes, She Heard

Stillness. Surrender. The soul's first whisper.

After the fire has passed, there is a silence that feels almost unfamiliar. The world pauses. The striving stops. And in the ashes of what once was, something sacred begins to stir. I remember seasons when life stripped everything away—roles, labels, certainty—leaving me with nothing to do but sit in the quiet and listen. It was there, in the stillness I once feared, that my soul finally had room to speak, and I had created space to listen.

This chapter holds stories of women who chose surrender over rushing forward and presence over distraction. In the quiet aftermath, they turned inward and heard the soft, unwavering whisper of truth guiding them home to themselves. This is the sacred in-between—the tender space between what was and what will be—where becoming begins and inner knowing is reborn.

The Other Shoe Dropping

KELLYANN SCHAEFER

For as long as I can remember, I've lived with the fear of the other shoe dropping. Correction—the "shoe dropping" came when things started to feel safe.

It began with worries around money: having enough, going broke, moving back to the "ghetto." Those fears made sense for someone who had clawed her way out of a hard life. But the bar kept moving. The younger, poorer version of me prayed for an extra $500 in the bank, which would feel safe. Then it was $1,000. The number kept growing: ten thousand, a hundred thousand. Each time I hit the "magic" safety number, the bar moved again. Not safe.

Eventually, the fears worsened and became irrational. Border-line psychotic at times. A simple walk with my dog could stop me in my tracks as my mind flooded with thoughts like, *"Don't get too comfortable ... your husband could die tomorrow. The house is about to catch on fire; your entire family is going to get into a car accident."* Completely unprovoked thoughts. Just random thoughts that felt real. The thoughts were vivid, relentless, and terrifying. No one I knew lived like this. I hid it.

A young girl who grew up in adversity, I had finally "arrived." I'd built everything I once dreamed of: a family, a husband who loved me, a reliable car, a beautiful home that looked like something from a magazine, and money in the bank. Everything that should have made me feel safe, secure.

Yet even with all the goodness I had achieved, I never fully relaxed. My mind filled with insidious whispers of everything that could go wrong ... a constant hum running in the background, preparing me for things to fall apart even when there was no reason to. I was always bracing for impact, expecting things to go sideways, scanning for danger in the quiet moments of life, mistaking hypervigilance for responsibility.

What I didn't understand was that fear didn't come out of nowhere. It was built in me. As a child, I had never learned what safety felt like. I learned survival.

While other kids were playing with dolls and coloring outside the lines, I was learning how to look after the kids. I'd stop them from walking down alleys, always anticipating danger and protecting myself and the people around me. I learned early that the world wasn't safe, and that if I didn't hold it together, everything might fall apart.

Maybe it was from watching my mother be beaten. At nine years old, running three blocks to the nearest pay phone to call 911 felt like saving her life. Or maybe it was the times our phone or electricity was turned off. Perhaps it was my boyfriend at fifteen, playing Russian roulette ... the click of the gun sending me bolting out the door.

So, I became good at protection. Probably too good. When you grow up like that, your body learns always to be prepared —reading people, situations, and energy before it even happens. Even when life becomes safe, that wiring doesn't just disappear. It hums underneath everything, whispering ... *Don't let your guard down. Something's coming.*

That's how I lived for decades, long after the danger was gone. Until one afternoon, driving alone, I heard a line from the audiobook playing through my car speakers: *"Parents need to be parents so that children can be children."*

The words landed like a jolt in my chest. I pulled to the side of the road, repeating them over and over, tears blurring my vision. I could hardly breathe … Something inside me cracked open. I finally felt seen. It was in that moment that I understood. The over-responsibility and lack of protection I carried as a child had shaped the woman I'd become. It made me resilient and capable … but it also shaped how I worked, how I loved, and how I moved through my life.

I built businesses, raised a family, checked every box with a smile. On the outside I looked confident and thriving, but underneath I was still scanning, protecting, bracing for impact. Control became my comfort, achievement my proof of safety. But no matter how much I achieved, it never quieted that voice. I'd climb one mountain and immediately start looking for the next.

When I finally did stop, everything in me revolted. Taking even an afternoon off came with guilt. That voice would start again. *You should be doing more. You're falling behind. You'll lose everything if you slow down.*

It's a strange thing to build a life that looks solid and successful, yet still feel like a small child inside, never sure what the future holds. I had the husband, the kids, the home, the money … all the things that were supposed to make me feel safe. For a brief moment, I believed I'd made it. But instead of peace, a new fear took hold … the fear of losing it all. The more secure life looked on the outside, the more terrified I became on the inside. My body didn't trust safety; it only trusted chaos and struggle.

I started therapy because I couldn't keep living in that constant state of internal panic. I told my therapist about my childhood, the life I had built, and the fears that haunted my mind and body. That's when I first heard the words complex post-traumatic stress disorder.

It wasn't weakness or that I didn't appreciate what I had. It was the body of a child who had learned to survive, now living in an adult world that looked safe but didn't feel safe yet. That's when healing began.

Healing didn't look like fireworks or breakthroughs. It looked like slowing down ... painfully, awkwardly, deliberately. Journaling each morning helped me meet myself on paper. Long walks reminded me I existed outside my thoughts. Solo travel taught me to be alone without feeling lonely. I learned to hug myself when I cried, placing a hand on my heart and whispering words I never heard as a child: *You're safe now. You did enough. You are enough.*

Healing also meant learning how trauma lives in the body and letting it move through me instead of locking it down. I learned to breathe again, to feel the weight of my own mind and not fear it, to recognize it for what it was.

Some days I still slip into old patterns, scanning the room, waiting for something to go wrong. But now I know ... it's only my nervous system remembering, not my intuition warning me.

I stopped making healing another goal. I stopped treating rest as a reward. Healing became less about fixing myself and more about coming home to myself.

There have been moments of grief for the childhood I didn't get to have, and deep gratitude for the little girl who kept me alive. She learned how to survive. Now I am learning how to live. Each small act of gentleness ... each walk, each journal page, each slow morning, has become a new kind of strength. The kind that doesn't come from pushing harder, but from allowing myself to be present with what I've created.

My work isn't done yet. But I feel freer now. Freer in my own awareness that I don't have to keep burning to prove I can rise. To show the world how resilient I am. Now I get to be me. The embers that once represented pain and protection have become reminders of resilience. I still feel them, warm, glowing, soft, but they don't consume me anymore. I still brace for impact sometimes, still feel that old ache of "not enough" trying to pull me back. But I can see it now. I can name it. I can remind that part of me ... You are SAFE, little one.

1. When in my own life have I mistaken survival for strength? Explore the moments you've called "being strong" that were really about staying safe, managing, or holding it all together.

2. What does "feeling safe" actually mean to me—and how do I know when I'm there? Many of us think safety comes from circumstances, but it often begins inside. Describe what safety feels like in your body.

3. What part of me thinks or feels like the other shoe will drop?

Beyond Duality: The Path to Wholeness

SANDY COMBS

As I was preparing to enter this incarnation, I must have said to my spirit guides and Source, "I want it ALL. From sorrow and self-loathing to rapturous love, and every emotion in between. Give me just enough danger to stay awake, challenges to test my gifts, and a path through darkness that awakens my creative power." I've often heard "be careful what you ask for." Yet now, on the other side of my heroine's journey, I wouldn't change a thing—though it wasn't always so. Let's take a closer look.

My early years were a living hell despite the appearance of privilege. Both of my parents carried the weight of mental illness and unresolved childhood trauma. My father appeared brilliant and accomplished and was admired by many. Like me, he was an only child. I knew he was proud to be my dad.

My mother was quieter, less certain of herself, her dreams mostly unspoken and projected onto my father. Her own childhood abuse had left unseen fractures in her psyche. When no one was around, she cast an icy glare at me, her eyes sharp with disgust and resentment. My daily need for nourishment and care was met with cold, silent indifference. While outwardly, my mother appeared mild and pleasant, I could sense her resentment toward me was growing. To cope, she distanced herself from me and quietly rejected the role of mother.

As an infant, I lay in my crib for hours, waiting for someone to feed, change, or comfort me as the days and nights blurred together. I cried until my small body gave way to exhaustion, only to awaken again to the empty silence. Unaware that my father traveled for work and was only home on weekends, my tiny nervous system adjusted quickly, and my intuition—still so new—was already awakened and growing sharper. My relentless cries must've weighed heavily on my mother, and at times I awoke with a pillow or blanket pressed against my face, breath stolen for moments that felt eternal. By six years old, I had already walked the edge of life and death twice, carrying within me the memory—and the quiet knowing that somehow, I was meant to survive.

I cannot remember a time when I couldn't hear other's thoughts or feel their emotions as if they were mine. From my earliest memories, I spoke with God and the angels, drawing from their presence a flowing stream of unconditional love. It was this constant source of love that I believe carried me through, enabling me to survive.

The hardest part of my early life wasn't my mother's rejection—I had never known anything different—it was the refusal of the adults around me to acknowledge my truth. When I tried to tell my dad about the horrible things my mother did to me in his absence, he insisted I was misunderstanding. Making matters worse, my mother hid her thoughts and actions from my dad, telling him how unmanageable and disobedient I was. Behind my dad's back, she smirked at me as cigarette smoke curled from her lips. I tried desperately to find common ground with my mother, only to be met with her refusal to acknowledge me.

For years, my ceaseless cries for help were dismissed. The more I tried to befriend my mother, the deeper her rejection grew and so did the anger within me. I found myself pondering ways to end the excruciating pain and rejection I faced daily, along with hideous thoughts of hate and destruction. One night, before my seventh birthday, standing in the doorway of my bedroom in our new home, I faced that darkness directly. I felt its presence with my entire being and then called on the love of my angels to fill my heart and body with pure love. As God's love permeated every cell of my body, I drew an invisible line across the threshold and declared out loud that my room be a haven of love. In that moment, I made a vow to God that I would always choose love over rage and hatred, and I asked for protection.

Throughout my developmental years, I swung back and forth like a pendulum, struggling to find my stability. The arts gave me fleeting refuge, yet beneath the surface depression and sorrow always lurked like shadows ready to drag me back to bed. Time and again, I fought to stay on this side of life. If I endured long enough, the darkness would break into ecstatic joy. In those moments, I felt unstoppable—alive with love, crystal clear mental clarity, and boundless creativity. I felt superhuman … until the inevitable crash left me feeling lifeless and bedridden. This cycle became the rhythm of my becoming. In search of my freedom, I devoured every self-help book my inner guidance offered. I pressed on with a flame of determination that could not be extinguished. Grateful for my relationship with Source and the ability to communicate with my angels, their voices assured me I would find my way through the storm and into the peace that was my birthright.

As adolescence pressed in, the question of who I was becoming grew heavier. My mother's neglect, compounded by my father's certainty that intellect and determination alone would be enough to ensure my success in life, became more than I could carry. Around this time, I began dating the quarterback of the football team. As I entered more of his world, I was introduced to recreational drugs, something I never imagined I would try. In the depths of my struggle, I found relief I never expected.

What began as curiosity soon became a turning point, carrying me into both escape and discovery. Fortunately for me, I was never addicted; recreational drugs calmed my nervous system and eased the near-daily desire to leave this earth. Once I left home, the anguish I had long endured diminished. The rhythmic highs and lows remained, but I was no longer trapped in a hostile environment, and I walked away from both the quarterback and the use of drugs.

With my newfound independence, I sought out psychologists and healers across a variety of modalities. As each layer of my struggle unraveled, I became more determined to uncover the root of my energetic imbalance. In time, I realized this quest was the foundation of my life's work. Though I occasionally needed the support of mild medications, I refused the heavy cocktail of pharmaceuticals the medical community insisted I needed. Deep inside, I knew I carried an energetic blueprint, and the more I followed it, the more it revealed my next step. Guided by this inner knowing, I moved into greater levels of balance and healing. Then, through what I can only call a series of miracles, I stumbled upon the name of a woman in a moment that sent chills racing through me. Within twenty-four hours, I had enrolled in her coaching program: one rooted in the wisdom of nature, the elements, and astrology.

My mentor teaches a powerful modality called the Inner Creation Team. This framework reveals the soul's elemental, astrological, and energetic blueprint: the unique composition of one's personality and energy. When I was introduced to this method, I knew I had found home within myself. Right before my eyes was the explanation of the highs and lows that others believed could only be managed with medication.

My entire soul lit up when I realized I was composed of all the fire archetypes in the zodiac, with three of them being in the most expansive sign of Sagittarius. Fire embodies spiritual

knowing, visibility, truth, and energetic action. Yet my blueprint also carries the deepest waters of the zodiac. Water governs emotions and feelings; it is often psychic, compassionate, and quietly nurturing. Unlike fire, water doesn't need visibility to thrive—it often prefers the still and unseen.

In that moment of revelation, I realized I wasn't broken. The fire within me yearned to shine; the water sought solace in the stillness. To see this truth reflected in my soul blueprint was life-changing. By embracing the elemental forces and aligning with nature's rhythmic cycles, I have learned to transmute challenge into wisdom and become the alchemist of my life. And I am passionate about helping others do the same.

Reflection

1. Is there a particular area in your life where you feel polarized? If so, how might you begin to hold them both with sacred curiosity rather than an either/or thought process?

2. Do you have a thought, feeling, or experience in your life that triggers strong emotions, such as shame or self-ridicule? How might simply shining light on it begin to soften your reaction?

3. Where might a subtle shift from avoidance to curiosity bring about a new perspective in your story?

A Sacred Space for Healing

JANNA LYNN WELLEMEYER

*L*et's start today's journey with a view of this beautiful, sacred place, Mount Shasta, California. Take some time to look at the mountain, the snowcapped top, the trees, and the clear blue skies surrounding her. Imagine being here, smelling the fresh pines, hearing the birds chirping, and feeling the sunshine warming your skin."

I'd been on my healing journey for about a year when I felt guided to join a group to learn about shamanism and more natural healing practices. I had heard of shamanism but didn't know much about it, other than that it is ancient wisdom from our ancestors. I loved the idea of more holistic healing methods, as I grew up as a very outdoors-loving person—yet through all my traumas, I had lost the ability to make nature a fun, relaxing, and regular part of my life.

"Now that you feel yourself in this sacred space, let's close our eyes and envision being there at the base of the mountain and seeing a small pathway leading off into the trees in front of you. Feeling adventurous, let's take that pathway as it winds deep into the forest."

After walking for a while, I began to climb in elevation, and I saw what appeared to be a well-lit cave entrance. This large cave looked inviting, so I walked into its mouth and was suddenly awed by the connection I felt to Mother Earth. This was a place of great healing, birthing, and change. As I looked around the cave, I saw the walls lined with handprints of all those women who came there before me. Red, black, brown, tan—painted handprints of the angel ancestors who are present with me that day to help my healing.

My heart and body felt deeply connected to that space: the cooler temperatures within the earthen cave, the musty smell of years gone by, and a hidden place of deep solitude. For the first time in a long time, I truly felt I was home. Home, among the trees, the birds, the sounds of nature, all cradling me gently within their arms, welcoming me back to my roots. Back to nature.

As I walked deeper into the cave, I came upon a beautiful, bright light, standing near two pools of water. Approaching the light, I felt a calming, welcoming feeling, and I saw it was Mother Earth, waiting for me. She gently took my hand and guided me into the first pool of water, the pool of release. In that pool, I intuitively heard her telling me to stand, listen to my body, and ask the waters to take away what I needed to leave behind.

I stood there, my eyes closed, and asked my body what she wanted me to leave behind. My heart clenched, tears welled within my eyes, and I heard, "Release all your fears."

Illness had forced itself into my life shortly after my youngest son was born with a heart murmur, which caused countless health scares in his early years. He also had seizures anytime he had fever-related illnesses. After having lost Jesse, my sweet, full-term, stillborn baby boy, I felt like a failure, like I was unable to care for a baby properly, as if I was being punished for trying again. I was full of fear, struggling every day to exist, while being overwhelmed with caring for my family.

I listed these fears: My fears of illness for myself and my family, my fears of failure, my fears of all the things left unsaid or undone, my fears of everything this life had thrown at me without offering me even the slightest sign of condolence. As tears streamed down, I physically felt a tingling sensation throughout my body, ending at my feet. I instantly knew I was being healed. Mother Earth allowed me a safe place to share all the things I'd been unable to share with anyone. My fears weren't evaporating because she was helping me; they left because I was brave enough to ask them to leave.

When I opened my eyes, Mother Earth guided me out of the first pool into the second one, the pool of attraction. Intuitively again, I heard her advise me that the pool was where we asked for what we would like in our lives. As someone who had forgotten what it felt like to dream, I hesitated to ask for anything. However, I took a deep breath before asking for continued good health for my family and me, and for abundance to flow in my life, both personally and in my healing business. I asked that my family could return to our home in Oregon, where we enjoyed living life more closely connected to the earth. (With my husband serving in the military, we had relocated to Oregon just a month after my stillborn loss, and it became the very foundation of where we all started healing as a family.)

As I finished my thoughts of attraction, I felt an overwhelming sense of happiness and joy take over my body, embracing me like a warm hug. Mother Earth smiled at me as if to signify that whatever I had asked for would be done. She then led me out of the second pool and back toward the mouth of the cave. I stopped at the handprints on the walls, where she gestured for me to leave my mark there for others to see. With red-brown paint, I left my handprint and felt a strong sense of connection with my ancestors.

As we reached the cave's mouth, Mother Earth embraced me and smiled before returning into the cave's depths. I stepped out and felt like a completely different person: lighter, freer. I followed the trail back to the base of the mountain and opened my eyes, coming back from our meditation.

That first guided shamanic meditation will always be such a

beautiful reminder of how blessed we truly are to have nature's healing powers at our fingertips. My healing journey has been a long, arduous process, as I've felt that I had to do it all alone. I'd worked one-on-one in a program that had already provided me great relief from the loss of Jesse and a few other traumas, but I hadn't really found anything that made me feel like I was returning to my true self. Loss seemed to have a way of gripping me, grabbing every part of my being so tightly that when I tried to let those trauma bonds go, I had entirely too much fear surrounding the question: "Who will I be without this part of me?"

I took a chance on shamanism, and I fell so deeply in love with the healing methods that I knew I had to learn more and share these experiences with other like-minded women who could open themselves enough to allow all the unhealed parts of themselves to heal. I've spent the last several months on many other journeys: learning who my spirit animals and spirit guides are, as well as visualizing where my sacred places are here on this beautiful earth. I'm forever grateful for these experiences; each journey holds its own sacred visions, locations, and healing opportunities.

Reflection

1. What fears or burdens have you been carrying that are ready to be released so you can step into greater freedom and healing?

2. Where—or with whom—do you feel most deeply connected to the healing energy of nature or spirit?

3. If you could leave your handprint on the wall of healing, what intention or message would you want it to carry for those who come after you?

Creating the Life I Want

APRIL SMALL

Growing up, I felt so alone that my heart raced when I was around others. When called on to speak, I choke. I couldn't understand why I felt so different from everyone around me. I didn't make friends easily; I didn't even really want to. I found ways to play by myself and made up elaborate imaginary worlds, and within them, stories of different lives and scenarios outside my own.

When you're young, you don't understand what's going on around you and why things are happening that scare you, hurt you, and make you feel unwanted.

I felt so overwhelmed by the outside world and the people around me that it was better to curl up inside my own head and use my imagination to take myself far away. This was how I dealt with those feelings. I just wanted to fly away and be someone else in my colorful, magical world, full of animals and big forests, where I was alone but happy and free.

One thing that shifted as I grew older was noticing that other people around me were suffering. I would see someone else cry or hurt, and I had an innate urge to help them. I didn't want anyone else ever to feel as sad and hurt as I had. One day, a girl came to school with a broken leg and was sitting in a wheelchair. I went right up and hugged her, and she became my very first friend. I'd had a hard time talking to other students before then, so I'd kept to myself. Seeing her stuck in that chair sparked something in me like a tiny ember. Later in life, I am so grateful for that moment, which I see was a small spark that led me down a much greater path than I could have ever imagined.

I started believing in others. I started recognizing that this world is a rough place and that we are all just thrown into the mix of whatever surroundings we're born into. We don't get to live alone in a magical forest with talking animals as best friends like I wanted to. But then I realized I wasn't the only person going through things—and it wasn't all about me, but rather about how I made others feel.

I wanted to be a lioness. I wanted to heal people's wounds, to make them laugh. I wanted to stand up for those being picked on and right any injustices I saw. I wanted to be brave enough to be myself, even though I dressed differently, thought differently, and was a little strange. I knew I wanted to help others.

As I grew older and worked different jobs, I met great people and learned so much—but I felt like I was missing something. I got bored and wasn't feeling aligned. I had forgotten about my life's purpose, although that small ember still burned inside me. I got sidetracked. Still in my twenties, I was wrapped up in life, boyfriends, going out, and—I admit—partying a bit too much and self-medicating, which I now regret.

I fell into a repeating cycle of bad choices, and I spiraled into another deep depression. I felt so alone that I attached to any-one who wanted me around, despite how they treated me. And I treated them poorly, too, because it was a very toxic time in my life. I had many regrets.

I was blessed to meet a friend at work who took me to a paint-n-sip for my birthday, and that night changed everything. We had so much fun—laughing, sipping wine—and my painting came out *terrible*. I joked, "I'm going to do this. I'm going to start my own business!" We laughed it off, but three months later I was putting in my notice and launching my own paint classes. It may have seemed fast, but something had sparked inside me. That night marked an important shift, pulling me into alignment with my passion.

Even though my business was going well, I was still stuck in cycles of toxic behavior and unhealthy habits. I found myself pregnant with my daughter and trapped in a painfully sour relationship. I felt like I was drowning—suffocating in the yelling, the anger, and the constant fear of what would happen when he came home. The anxiety dragged up old memories from childhood. I wanted a better life for my daughter, the way all parents do. We always hope to do better for our children than what we experienced.

I stayed far too long. By the time my daughter was four, I had become a physical wreck. My heart never stopped racing. I looked awful and had stopped trying to hide it. I simply didn't care anymore. I felt like I was walking on eggshells every moment he was home. I couldn't take any more. Every fiber of my being was screaming. I felt like a little kid again—choking. I had to get out of the box I felt trapped in.

One day, I sat there crying—again—but something was different. This time I knew I was done. I knew I couldn't do this anymore. I needed to end the relationship and find my way back to joy. I had lost nearly all of my creativity. Living in that cycle of negativity had drained me of inspiration. Deep down, I knew it was time to start saying no to anything that didn't bring me closer to alignment with my purpose and my joy.

So I began removing things from my life that weren't aligned—starting with my relationship with my daughter's father. It wasn't healthy for either of us, and I couldn't keep living that way and expect things to magically improve. Next came healthier habits—simple things like going for walks and spending more time in nature. With each day, I could feel life returning to me.

The most important shift was feeling my spark come back. I felt tingles in my body and these beautiful, random ideas and words of inspiration started showing up again. I could hear my inner creative voice—my higher self—whispering to me. The light was returning. I reached for a paintbrush and let everything pour onto the canvas. I kept returning to that canvas, and with each new piece of art and each sunny day, my joy flowed back. When I say leaving was the best choice I ever made, I mean it.

I needed to release myself from everything that no longer served me. I needed to step back into my power, reconnect with the inner lioness I had lost touch with, and I needed to do it not just for myself but for my daughter. I didn't want her childhood filled with yelling and drama. I wanted her to have peace—to run free and play. I wanted to enjoy my time with her and show her my true self, not the empty version I had become. I wanted to shine for her so she could see what's possible—and to remind myself of that, too.

We have to create the lives we want. It starts with filling our own cups, but it's also about what we do with the energy and life we've reclaimed—what imprint we leave on the world. So I stepped back into my lioness. I protected my joy and my baby, and I led with love, hoping to spread creativity and inspiration into the world around me.

Reflection

1. What parts of yourself—your creativity, voice, or inner "lioness"—have you abandoned, and what would it look like to reclaim them now?

2. When have you stayed in a situation too long out of fear, habit, or self-doubt—and what finally helped you choose yourself?

3. What small embers of joy or inspiration are flickering in your life right now, waiting for you to notice and nurture them?

The Spark That Called Me Back

REV. FELICIA MESSINA-D'HAITI

"Be ready" was the message that kept popping up in my mind. First, it was a quiet whisper. My first thought was, "Be ready for what?" It didn't seem urgent, so I put it to the side. A couple of months went by. Then, after I completed the ministerial program that I was enrolled in, I heard it again. This time it was a bit louder: "Be ready." I sat with what it could mean and looked for signs to reveal themselves.

There had been many unsettling events in the workplace. Though the program I managed had been expanding to new schools at a good pace, funds for essential resources were being eliminated each year. The budget for the upcoming year had been kept secret, which was highly unusual. When I asked questions about the upcoming year, I was told I needed to wait.

At the same time, I had expressed on several occasions that I missed teaching. I had worked in the field of public education for more than twenty-six years and taught art, art history, and enrichment classes in public middle schools for just over ten of those years. My last year teaching had been the year I was recovering from stage 3B colon cancer and the cancer treatments. The last year of teaching, I struggled to make it through the day, experiencing low energy levels and lingering brain fog. My body needed a rest, and a position working in an office supporting teachers opened at exactly the right time.

During the time I worked in the office, there had been several rounds of budget cuts. During these times, I had a feeling of safety since I was the only person in the organization doing the work of supporting enrichment teachers and gifted programming and helping to grow these programs in the school district. My job and its more flexible hours also supported my continued healing, medical appointments, and my personal and ministerial studies. Although I enjoyed the work, I was not being challenged to grow. And though the program was expanding, its growth was inconsistent. Every time I took a step forward, I was pushed several steps back.

The message to "be ready" also came up in the ministerial program. And although I always connected it to being spiritually ready, I also felt it applied to my work situation. When I started the office position, I told myself that I would be there until I retired or decided to leave to become a full-time entrepreneur, so I was not looking for a new position.

In early summer, after the repeated "be ready" messages, I made the decision to renew my teaching and administrator licenses so I could be ready for whatever was to come. I stumbled upon a set of asynchronous classes at a great price and registered immediately. Yet I did not start the classes. I must admit that I was tired of taking classes and resisted starting these. The past several years, I had been enrolled in an intense program along with treatment for two different cancer diagnoses. I wanted to rest; yet each time I pushed the classes aside, I could hear that little whisper: "Be ready." As I started taking the courses, I also applied to be part of a teacher applicant pool so I could view new opportunities. I did not believe that my position would be eliminated, yet I felt the urge to explore this path.

When I first looked at open positions, there were only one or two in the visual arts, so I told myself maybe this was for me in another year. Then, unexpectedly, a few days later, I received two separate phone calls from principals who had seen my name in the pool. I was invited to interviews for positions that had not yet been listed. I went to both schools, which were amazing in different ways. I was offered both positions, so I prayed and meditated about which opportunity to accept. Ultimately, I felt that my soul was calling me back to work with middle school students. I spoke to the principals in the morning. I remember that it was a Tuesday morning because that same afternoon, I was called into a meeting on the top floor of our building, where I was told that my position had not been included in the upcoming budget. The meeting invitation contained no details, but I immediately knew what it was for. My supervisor accompanied me to meet with the chief of our division, who read from a script informing me that my position had been eliminated.

Knowing that the budget is always created in the fall and approved in the early winter months, I was saddened to realize that they had known they would take this action for more than six months, yet they told me nothing.

I also felt glad that I listened to what Spirit had been telling me and was ready when the time came. I looked at my new position with mixed feelings. I was so excited about stepping back into being an art teacher. I loved teaching and seeing students light up when they were given opportunities to be creative in school. I felt like this shift had been calling me for a long time.

A wonderful synchronicity is that in the few months before this decision, I had started addressing some health concerns that had popped up after recovering from the cancer diagnoses I experienced. I started releasing weight, gained more energy, and was able to be on my feet more. The brain fog and other body aches and pains had dramatically cleared as well.

As I spent time closing out my current position, I began to experience feelings of grief and loss. Even though I had chosen to shift jobs, it was clear that some shift was going to happen, even without me making that decision.

Although I witnessed how the supervisors put little thought into the continuity and fidelity of the program I managed and the community that I was a central part of, I was also excited about teaching again. I felt so strongly that I made the right decision for myself and what Spirit was guiding me to do.

I readied myself for the shift. In less than four weeks, I completed the recertification courses, closed out my current position, and jumped into the new one. And although I was fully confident that this was the right choice, I experienced a great deal of sadness during the sudden change, as I felt like part of my identity had suddenly been ripped away from me. I also began to examine how I felt when I left the previous teaching position thirteen years ago. Even though I knew it was best for me at the time, I never acknowledged my grief about leaving. I had always enjoyed teaching middle school–aged children; yet a major reason why I left was to provide a better space for me to heal from surgeries and chemotherapy treatments. I felt like I had no choice at the time. My body needed the support, but I was sad to leave.

Then, in the years following my departure from teaching, my life took a different turn. Two more cancer diagnoses arrived, each one demanding its own cycle of treatment, recovery, and resilience. My body carried the marks of surgeries and treatments, each scar a reminder of what I had endured and survived. As I reflect on these experiences, I see how they prepared me for my return to teaching with new awareness and expectations for my own self-care while I stepped into a challenging role. I am ready to honor myself and my body as I provide safe and creative spaces for children.

Over the last few years, there have been moments when I questioned whether I would ever have the stamina to return to a classroom. Teaching requires energy, presence, and a kind of steady strength that illness can sometimes strip away. Still, the desire never left me. I knew that I would not be guided in this direction unless it was the right path for me now. And now, I know that I am ready.

As I step into this new chapter, heeding this call to be ready, I carry both the fragility and the strength of what I've been through. There is a deep sense of release, as if chains I didn't even realize I had been carrying have finally fallen away. It feels as though I have been freed from a prison of limitation and of waiting. For the first time in years, I am stepping forward not out of obligation, but out of choice, ready to return to the work that always felt like home.

Reflection

1. When has your inner voice—or a quiet spiritual nudge—asked you to "be ready," and how did you respond?

2. What endings in your life have actually been beginnings in disguise, guiding you toward work or purpose that feels more like home?

3. How have your hardest experiences—illness, loss, uncertainty—prepared you to return to something you love with deeper clarity and strength?

The Return of the Spark

Reclaiming your voice, worth, and inner knowing.

There comes a moment—sometimes subtle, sometimes thunderous—when a woman feels herself come back in alignment with herself. I remember the first time I spoke a truth I had been swallowing for decades, the moment my body exhaled, and my soul whispered, *This is who you are.*

It wasn't loud, but it was unmistakable. The spark had returned. In that moment, I had reclaimed my light and my truth, and there was no turning back. This chapter gathers stories of remembrance—when women began to trust what they knew in their bones, reclaim their voice, and draw new boundaries rooted in self-worth. A quiet *no* became a powerful yes to themselves. Their intuition sharpened and their confidence stirred. The spark that once flickered beneath the ashes is no longer hidden. It is rising, asking to be honored, expressed, and lived. This is the moment a woman remembers she was never meant to stay small.

The Lie That Led Me to Truth

KIM GORE

I had just told the biggest lie of my life.

Sitting in an armchair in exam room 2, I watched my doctor and friend, Dr. Bonnita Portier, finish typing her notes. She glanced up, eyes sharp with curiosity, and asked, "Why are you working construction? There are plenty of body-friendly jobs more suited to you. Your body needs a break. You're a smart woman."

Handing me a lab slip, with quiet authority, she said three words that shook me to my core: "Go to college."

Those words terrified me. My work has always been technical, never academic. "What?" I laughed nervously. "No way. I'm not going to college."

Her tone softened but stayed steady. "There is no reason you can't."

"I'm fifty years old. I need to work. I can't afford to start over."

She held my gaze a beat longer. "What are you afraid of?"

The honest answer burned inside me, but I couldn't speak it. Silence filled the room; an hour had passed since she asked the question. Finally, to ease the weight of her expectation, I promised to go to college.

It was the biggest lie I had ever told.

Old memories crowded in of third grade. The school planned

to advance me to fourth grade, since my grades were above average. My mom challenged the principal, then appealed the school's decision to the Board of Education with her voice echoing, *"But the girl can't read!"* This resulted in me being held back while other kids moved on. The humiliation of that moment still coursed through my veins.

In sixth grade, I was adrift. My parents had recently divorced, and the safe little world I once knew splintered apart. We moved uptown to a small apartment, away from the familiar rhythm of neighborhood friends. I felt unmoored, like nothing fit anymore.

Amid the upheaval, two teachers became lifelines. My physical education teacher noticed me—really saw me—when I felt invisible everywhere else. We talked before and after class, and those conversations gave me a place to breathe. Movement, games, and the chance to release bottled-up energy grounded me. My English teacher offered extra support in class, patient guidance when words tangled. She never made me feel small, only capable.

Those relationships steadied me when my home life felt like quicksand. They reminded me that I wasn't completely lost. By seventh and eighth grade, I found my spark again. I was popular, known as athletic and funny. When I received the "Most Improved in English" award twice, I soared. No one knew the battles I fought with reading, but in those moments, I was high on hope, proof that effort could bloom into pride.

High school, however, took a turn downward. On paper, I looked successful: honor roll student, two-sport athlete. But inside, I carried the heavy weight of failure. The Maryland Functional Reading Test became my nemesis. I failed it once. Then again. The third time I finally passed, but only because it was read aloud to me. My score of 86 percent should have felt like victory, yet instead I thought, *So I'm not completely dumb … just somewhat stupid.*

The lowest point came when Mom and I walked into a high school conference room where five teachers and administrators sat waiting to share my test results. My stomach sank. I felt exposed, as if my secret had been dragged into the light. *They all know now,* I thought. *My life in high school is over.* I told them about the nights I stayed up until four in the morning trying to finish assignments, about how I frantically read ahead in class to avoid humiliation. I wasn't learning; I was surviving.

Specialized testing confirmed it: dyslexia. My schedule was changed, and I was placed in "special" reading classes with the agreement of my mother. Sitting by those large classroom windows, I turned my head so others wouldn't see me. I didn't want to be marked as dumb. One teacher sealed it with certainty: "You are not college material. You won't amount to much. You'll probably end up working in a factory like your mom." Her words branded me, and I carried that label long into adulthood.

So, when Dr. Portier, years later, asked, "What are you afraid of?" I didn't dare say the truth: I was terrified of failing again, of being laughed at, of hearing that inner child's voice still calling me stupid. Instead, I nodded and promised I'd go to college. Outwardly brave, but inside, I knew I was lying.

When I told my wife, a lifelong educator and school counselor, about my "lie," she didn't blink. Suddenly, the money, the time, the how … none of it mattered to her. She simply said, "Let's check it out." Within days, she had arranged visits to two community colleges. A week later, with the help of a grant and a part-time job, I was enrolled.

To my surprise, the learning disabilities coordinator welcomed me with open arms, easing my fears and setting up support: audiobooks, extended testing time, small-group exams, and math and writing labs. For the first time in my academic life, I wasn't battling alone. My wife and this coordinator became my lifelines and my champions.

Two years later, I walked across the stage with an associate's degree, with honors. The moment was surreal. I hadn't walked at my high school graduation because I attended summer school to finish a year early. This ceremony felt like redemption. As my family watched, I held my head high.

At fifty years old, I finally discovered that I was capable. More than capable, I loved learning. Physics, of all things, lit me up inside. That newfound confidence nudged me to apply to a state school for echocardiography ultrasound, and to my astonishment, I was accepted. Science, a path I never would have imagined for myself, became the place I stretched wings I didn't know I had.

My motivation was deeply personal. Both of my parents had cardiac issues, and I wanted to understand, to help, to advocate. With the same accommodations, I completed the program and passed the national physics exam. Though I never pursued the career formally, my training had purpose. I kept my mom alive longer by asking doctors the extra questions others might have skipped, trusting my instincts when a procedure didn't feel right, and insisting on alternatives that gave her precious additional years of quality life.

Looking back, I realize promising to go to college wasn't the lie I thought it was. It was the first crack in the wall I had built around myself. What once felt like a bluff turned out to be a blessing. Dr. Portier saw something in me I couldn't yet see. Her belief planted the seed. My wife and my community college nurtured it. And finally, I found the courage to water it.

More than ten years later, I see how pivotal that moment was. I learned to open myself to possibility, to peel back the labels that had limited me, to stop making myself a victim of circumstance. My new approach to life embraces freedom in all forms, knowing that dreams can be achieved with support, community, and, most of all, belief in myself.

Today, my wife and I travel full-time in our rolling home, exploring new adventures and connecting with women who are expanding their own dreams. Our success is built on mutual support and owning our gifts, just as we encourage others to do.

That one moment in an exam room changed the trajectory of my life. The girl who was told she wasn't smart enough, wasn't college material, who was destined for the shoe factory … she rose. And the woman she became discovered not only her wings, but the freedom to fly.

Reflection

1. Think of a time when you told yourself a "lie" (like *I can't*, *I'm not enough*, or *I'll never …*). What truth might have been hiding underneath that fear?

2. Who in your life has "seen" you—really noticed your worth—at a time you felt invisible? How did their belief in you shift your perspective?

3. What cracks have appeared in your own "wall of self-doubt"? How could you water the seeds of possibility shining through?

Rewriting the "Shoulds"

YVETTE LEFLORE

I stood looking between the trainer at the gym and the calendar on my phone, feeling the heat of it in my palm and stress in my shoulders. Should I book my first one-on-one on the anniversary of his death, or find someone else for breakfast?

Weeks before, thoughts of what I should do on this anniversary kept creeping in. Whether I was on a walk, watching TV, or sitting quietly, I'd hear the questions: "What should I do to honor my husband on the anniversary of his death? What would be appropriate to mark my first year without him?" I'd heard from so many others, and in all the literature, about the difficulties of the firsts: the holidays, birthdays, anniversaries, and especially the one-year mark. I'd been anticipating how challenging the day would be.

Ideas of what to do and how to honor him, me, and us whirled through my mind. Perhaps going out for a meal at one of our favorite restaurants would work. Should I take a walk near the river where we used to spend time together? Maybe I'd feed the ducks and geese like we did when he was too weak to walk. I thought about spreading his ashes somewhere meaningful. Briefly, I even considered watching the news because he loved it—but I quickly took that off the list.

One thing I knew: I didn't want to work. I wanted space to feel whatever surfaced that day. That was an easy decision, so I took the date off my booking calendar.

I also knew I wanted some self-care, so I booked a massage.

Then the idea struck—I wanted to go out to breakfast and have his favorite meal: French toast and sausage. Now the question was, who to invite? I needed a friend I could laugh and maybe even cry with. Someone who wouldn't use that sing-songy, "How are you to-day?" voice. Someone who could balance memories of the past, presence in the moment, and conversation about the future. Someone who wouldn't coddle me but would comfort me. Someone I could chat with and maybe even forget the day's significance.

Where would I spread his ashes? I thought of the places we'd been and settled on a garden trail we used to walk and bird-watch. We'd found the trail one spring after moving from New York to Virginia. The azaleas were blooming in all their glory with pink, red, and white bursting forth as the bees busily pollinated. We discovered birds we'd never seen before. I smiled remembering how we used the Merlin Bird ID app to identify an American redstart, then found it in the trees with our binoculars. It had such a special energy. It would be the perfect place to spend time with his spirit and honor mine.

I put off reaching out to my friend about breakfast, and when I finally did, she wasn't available. I struggled to think of who else to ask. I had plenty of people, but no one else felt quite right.

So, there I stood in a quandary, looking between my calendar and the trainer's face. In a matter of seconds, I ran through the options of choosing another day or another friend. I chose neither and booked my first appointment for the morning of the anniversary.

The night before the appointment, I was just about asleep when I remembered a conversation we'd had about a month and a half before he died. I sat on the side of the hospital bed in our living room, holding his hand.

"I was thinking. You know that bench down by the river where we sit? The place where we saw that indigo bunting?"

"Yeah, why?" he replied.

"What if we make that a place we meet once you transition? I've been told that I can create the strong visual of it and include all the senses, and while I'm in a dream state, we can sit on that bench and have a conversation. What do you think?"

He looked at me with thoughtful eyes. "I think we can do that."

It had been a year, and I'd forgotten all about that conversation. So, the night before the one-year anniversary, I set the intention that we'd meet on the bench. I went to sleep conjuring every detail of the area, excited to see him. When I awoke, we hadn't connected.

On the anniversary day, I decided not to spread the ashes. Instead, I took some time for a quiet morning before my 8:00 a.m. gym appointment. I walked into the gym carrying the weight of years of perceived fitness failure. I hadn't worked out in seven years and carried a lifetime of body-shaming messages. As I waited, the upbeat music of a class drowned out the sounds of exertion but not my inner critic. Agitation and doubt rippled through me.

As the trainer took me through the weights and machines, that sense of failure began to melt. Yes, I was only lifting twenty pounds, but I was there! There was something magical about choosing to honor my body with a workout rather than eating a carb-filled breakfast.

As I left the gym—elated, sweaty, and full of pride—I heard a crow call. As a birder and someone attuned to animal messages, I always pay attention to bird calls. I wondered what message it had for me. I looked up at the brilliant blue sky filled with white cumulus clouds and felt the warmth of the sun pour down. I followed the sound of the crow until I spotted it: Above the trees, in that gorgeous blue sky, circled a majestic hawk.

My husband had an affinity for hawks and had visited me as one many times since he died. Here he was again, circling above, applauding my choice of the gym over French toast.

I leaned against my car, feeling its warmth, and watched the hawk circle as the emotions spilled forth. I cried with gratitude that he was cheering from above. I cried because I still missed his physical presence. I cried because the tears were simply there to cry. I stayed until all the emotions had spilled out and the hawk had moved on. Then I sat in my car, breathing deeply to return to my body.

After that magical moment, I went for my massage. I snuggled under the blankets with a warm heating pad beneath me while my back was massaged with hot stones. As I relished the sensations, I slipped into that sleep-like state I often reach during massages.

Then I heard my husband call my name: "Yvette!" It sounded like he was calling me from another room, beckoning me to pay attention.

I startled out of that restful state, confused, until I realized what had happened. I'd entered that in-between space where Spirit can easily communicate with us. Another magical moment where my husband came to say, "Hello, I'm still here. Good job taking care of yourself!" This time, I smiled instead of crying.

Throughout the day, people reached out to check on me. They asked with a bit of trepidation and lots of love, "How are you doing?"

I told them all that I felt awesome.

All day, I had that giddy, high feeling I get when everything is going my way. My body vibrated with energy and joy. I'd be in the middle of something and notice that I was smiling. How could that be? It was the one-year anniversary of my husband's death, and I was happy. Giddy? Naturally high? A bit of doubt crept in. What's wrong with me? Why was I not reeling with the emotion I'm "supposed" to be feeling today?

Later that night, I reflected on the day and all the amazing experiences—going to the gym, seeing the hawk, hearing my husband's voice, listening to my intuition, feeling joy—and then I got it. I was rewriting the "shoulds" of the anniversary. Taking care of myself, being joyful, and staying open to his signs were the best ways to honor him.

I felt free from the constraints of grief and the "shoulds" I'd been told about. A month earlier, I thought I'd spend most of the day in tears and mourning. Instead, I found myself steeped in joy. I'd rewritten what the day had to look like—and it felt amazing.

1. When life offers you a choice between following an old pattern or trying something new, what helps you lean toward the path that nurtures you most?

2. What "shoulds" in your life are you ready to release so you can write your own path?

3. Think about a time when you felt an unexpected moment of joy in the midst of grief or difficulty. What did it show you about your own resilience?

House of Mirrors

LEE MURPHY WOLF

The cursor on my laptop screen blinked as I stared at the blank page. My article was overdue, and I had a wicked case of writer's block. Sighing, I looked out the window of my brother-in-law's apartment. It was a crisp December morning. As I watched the sun dance across the Hudson River, my mind started to drift.

I sank deeper into the couch and felt the heaviness of the last six months catch up with me. Over the summer, my husband, Mark, and I decided to rent out our home in Florida and move back to Vermont. Turning our property into a rental had been more complex than we expected. Our house in Vermont was in disarray, with stacks of boxes everywhere waiting to be unpacked. I felt ungrounded and struggled to focus.

Mark wasn't himself lately either. He was jumpy and easily triggered. Sometimes I could feel him quivering in his sleep. As I'd lie awake listening to his breath, I would gently touch his shoulder to try to soothe him. In the morning, I'd ask if everything was okay, and he would assure me that it was. But intuitively, I *knew* something was wrong. In almost fifteen years of marriage, we had never held back from each other. What was it, and why was he afraid to tell me?

My stream of consciousness was interrupted by the sound of Mark's feet shuffling across the living room floor. He approached me gingerly and asked, "Is this a good time? I want to talk to you about something."

I saved my blank document and closed my laptop. My stomach was in knots, but I made eye contact and calmly said, "Yes, you can always talk to me about anything."

Mark paused for what seemed like an eternity. Then he blurted out, "We are the victims of wire fraud."

I felt a wave of intense pain rip through me, tears stinging my eyes. The word *victim* cut deep, as if I had stepped down on shards of broken glass.

I felt like I was riding an emotional roller coaster. My sense of trust and safety was shaken to the core. My parents were never great with money, and I grew up in a "feast or famine" household. Either there was plenty of money, or barely enough to pay the bills. I was taught at a young age that scarcity was something to fear and that people who had money were either born with it or had good luck. Above all else, I was taught that I must create financial security to survive.

Throughout our marriage, Mark and I had been blessed with a loving relationship and financial abundance. Now someone had taken hundreds of thousands of dollars that we had not authorized. Mark said no one was returning his calls, and if the situation wasn't resolved quickly, the company could foreclose on our home. I felt helpless. I had never doubted our financial decisions before, and I started to wonder if I had been lulled into a false sense of security that was about to come crashing down.

My self-preservationist instincts kicked into high gear. When I was feeling raw and vulnerable, I'd lash out at my husband, blaming him for taking out such a large credit line or accusing him of not trusting me. I knew in my heart that he was just trying to protect me, but emotionally, I had no control over what would fly out of my mouth at any given moment. I didn't like this harsh side of myself and worried that if I didn't get a grip on it, it would damage our marriage.

In other moments, I was overcome with guilt. It had been my idea to invest in real estate, which was why we had taken out a home equity line of credit in the first place. What had I done, and had my desires put us at risk?

Then my anger bubbled up. We were supposed to leave for Portugal soon. We wanted to know what it would be like to live there and had rented an apartment for three months. Was that the right thing to do when we had no answers, and it seemed like no one was going to help us?

I talked to a close friend about the situation. After a long pause, he said, "I can't believe I am hearing this. You and Mark are always on top of things. If this could happen to you, it could happen to anybody."

I let that sink in. My friend was very successful, and I admired his business acumen. I had no idea he perceived Mark and me that way. Maybe this wasn't my fault after all. I started to come down off my ledge and felt less emotionally charged.

Mark reached out to friends as well. When he told his story, he always led with, "We are the victims of wire fraud." The more I heard him say it, the odder it sounded.

My thoughts and emotions swirled as I tried to make sense of it. Just a few days ago, I felt like I would throw up every time I heard the "v" word. Now I felt light and spacious inside, almost serenely calm. If I were a victim, why wasn't I panicking? Shouldn't I be falling apart?

It was as if I had just walked into a house of mirrors and, for the first time, could see my distorted view of myself. Snippets of family mishaps, romances gone awry, and personal traumas involving money ran through my mind. I saw moments when I had been financially irresponsible, moments when I had enabled other people's poor financial choices, and moments when I had given up on myself too soon because I was terrified of becoming financially destitute.

But this was different. The reflection looking back at me from the funhouse mirror was not a vibrational match for who I was now. This wire fraud incident was not connected to these old patterns, nor had I caused it. That long-held view of myself was outdated, and it was time to let her go. Seeing it all so clearly was disorienting and liberating.

While driving back home from the train station, I shared my light bulb moment with Mark. I said, "Honey, we were victimized by someone, but we are not victims."

As he took that in, his body relaxed, and he became lighter. Then he said, "You're right."

Once I let go of that old victim energy, everything started to shift. Communication between Mark and me started to flow again. We talked about our fears and worked through them together so we could lessen their grip and let them go. A close friend suggested we hire a lawyer, and we did, finding someone highly skilled to help us.

With the right support in place, we focused on the next decision: Was this the right time to go to Portugal? We talked about what we wanted and what we believed. We knew in our hearts that the Universe had our backs, that this mess may take time to clean up, and that we would be made whole. We also agreed that the most important thing we could do was to create momentum for our lives by sticking with our plans. It was a clear yes.

We were sitting in the airport lounge an hour before takeoff when our attorney called. He told us that we were not being held responsible for the unauthorized amount and that our credit scores would be restored.

We popped a bottle of champagne to celebrate. As I watched the bubbles fizz, I exhaled a sigh of relief. Mark and I looked into each other's eyes and clinked glasses. I took a slow sip. The champagne was delightfully cool and crisp. I smiled softly and savored the sweetness of the moment.

Reflection

1. When has a crisis or unexpected challenge revealed
an outdated story you'd been telling yourself—and what
shifted once you saw the truth more clearly?

2. How do your earliest beliefs about money, safety, or
scarcity still influence your reactions today—and which
of those beliefs are ready to be released?

3. When has honest communication—either with
yourself or someone you love—transformed a situation
that once felt overwhelming?

How I Became a Radio Psychic

SHA BLACKBURN

I have been psychic for as long as I can remember. When I was less than ten years old, I only used my intuition and the voice of my soul to speak my "wisdom." And when I turned twelve, an older neighbor from up the street gave me the Gypsy Witch Fortune Telling Cards because she thought I would get a kick out of them. I sure did! I progressed to the tarot in my mid-teens and began a more earnest career through my late high school and college years. My belief in my psychic abilities rarely wavered; they always seemed part of who I am.

When I became a mom at twenty-three, my husband was not thrilled with my psychic–witchy self, and I put this part of myself on the back burner of my life for a few years. But when we split, I realized I had to raise my son alone. I needed a side hustle to shore up my income—something I could do at my own pace and when I was available. That's why I returned to psychic fairs and working out of little new age shops.

As I dove back into leveraging my psychic abilities, I met a man who worked at one of the shops where I did readings, and we became the very best of friends. We had breakfast every Saturday morning, shared secrets, and gossiped. He later opened his own business and began advertising on a local radio station.

One day in 2004, I got an early morning panicked phone call from my friend. His truck had broken down, and he had an appointment that he needed to be at for 8:00 a.m. I had that day off and offered to give him a ride. I never asked where he was going; he just provided directions as I drove. As we approached our destination, I saw an unassuming strip center that had seen better days. It housed a collection of random businesses: a coffee shop, a daycare, a radio station office, and a liquor store. Quite the odd combination of places! We pulled into the plaza when he announced that he was scheduled to do readings on live radio! *How interesting!* I felt excited for him to have that opportunity.

"Come in with me. I'll introduce you to the radio DJs," he said. So, I did.

We entered the studio, and beyond the tiny welcome area was a maze of offices and sound rooms. It felt very quiet, almost eerily quiet. The on-air personalities came out to greet us. I was introduced as "The LoonWitch," my stage name. They asked if I also read the tarot, and I said I did.

"Would you consider joining us on-air to do some readings?" one of them asked.

Those who know me well say that I can be reserved. My heart pounded. *Me? On live radio?* All of my previous readings had been in person. I didn't know how it would work to do a reading for someone over the phone, let alone being live on the radio! My friend eagerly agreed to do so. And there I was: walking into a small room with acoustic tiling on the wall, a huge control panel, and only enough room to walk in and take my seat on a stool. There were three "stations" for the DJs and guests to sit at, each with its own headset and microphone. Once we donned our headphones and the microphones were adjusted, it was my turn to be introduced to the vast network of listeners on a Friday morning FM drive-time show.

I always have my tarot deck with me. They are my dearest

friends, and I often consult with them when I need guidance and support. I had pulled a card for myself when we first entered the broadcast studio quietly to bolster my courage, or to know if I should run for the hills. The card that I pulled was the major arcana card, "The High Priestess." The High Priestess represents the power, the higher self, and the guide who knows your secrets and knows only to answer the questions asked. She is a very spiritual and intuitive being. I felt buoyed by her as the answer to my question of whether I could give live readings on the radio.

My first experience of reading on live radio was terrifying and exhilarating all at the same time. The first reading I did made the caller cry happy tears. Though I don't remember the question she asked, I remember her reaction and how everyone in the radio studio was silent and almost awestruck by my accuracy. I felt impressed by myself as well!

In practice, I go into every reading with no expectation other than that my client will receive the information they need, even if it's not the information they want to hear. When I can provide clear and specific information for them with precision and accuracy, it's always a thrill—kind of like a pat on the back from the Universe, reminding me that this is something beautiful that I should keep doing.

At the end of that first show, I was invited back.

I continued being a guest on that same show for twelve years, once a month on a Friday morning. And since then, I have been on multiple radio shows and podcasts as a guest reader. As of this writing, I have built a thriving business as a psychic and spiritual coach, serving global clients from nineteen countries (so far).

Who knew that helping a friend in a moment of need would lead not only to one interesting experience, but also to a fantastic opportunity to create a truly remarkable life? When opportunity knocks, remember to say, "Yes!"

Reflection

1. When has following an unexpected nudge—or
helping someone in a moment of need—opened a door
you never could have planned for?

2. What parts of your authentic self have you tucked
away to fit someone else's comfort—and what might
happen if you brought them back into the light?

3. Where in your life is the Universe asking you to trust
your intuition and say "yes" to something that both
excites and scares you?

Soul Whispers + Surrender = The Way Forward

ANDRA EVANS

What do you do when your soul starts to stir—right in the middle of a meeting? There I was, sitting at a boardroom table, watching a presentation, when something inside me whispered, *Pay attention*. At first, I ignored it. But soon, a tiny earthquake began to rumble through my nervous system. I tried to appear composed, yet inside I felt restless, unsettled, and strangely awake.

When the meeting ended, I returned to my desk, and everything looked suddenly foreign. My familiar surroundings—the desk, the computer, the framed photos—seemed to belong to someone else. I took a deep breath and tried to anchor myself back into work, but that inner tremor wouldn't quiet. A knowing washed over me: I didn't belong there anymore. Not in that role, and not in that world.

My career had been a steady climb through communications—from nonprofit animal welfare into the fast-paced realm of technology, where I worked in change management communications. At first, it was exciting and rewarding. But after seven years, I had to admit that the tech world felt dizzying and disconnected from my heart. What I really wanted was to help people—directly, deeply.

Within weeks, that inner restlessness grew louder. My company began restructuring after a merger, and I could no longer see my future there. So, with a deep breath and shaky hands, I resigned, taking my stock options with me. The act of quitting sent a rush of adrenaline through my body—part exhilaration, part terror. I was proud, yes, but also terrified. My favorite manager gave me a knowing smile and said, "Leap, and the net will appear."

Her words carried me forward, but I had no idea the leap would send me spiraling into an identity crisis—a dark night of the soul. I had always nurtured a quiet spiritual life, but now, without my job to define me, my inner world came alive. I began having vivid dreams, sensations, even inner voices that seemed to guide me. *Was this my soul?* I called them "soul whispers," though at times I wondered if I was losing my mind. Had I ruined my career? Was this a midlife crisis?

Around that time, I was reading about spiritual surrender. Something bigger was happening, and I decided to stop resisting. I began confiding in trusted mentors who reassured me that I was, indeed, being called. My calling was calling me.

Soon, that inner guidance urged me to move back to my hometown and return to my first love—psychology. Although the decision felt right, self-doubt followed close behind. I kept asking myself, *What am I doing with my life?* I moved home as winter arrived, with no place to live except my mother's house. Living once again in my childhood home felt heavy, as though I were moving backward. But it also became a catalyst. Old wounds resurfaced in the mother-daughter dynamic, demanding healing and compassion.

Despite the discomfort, I was grateful for a soft landing and a familiar place to regroup. I sensed that this upheaval had something to do with my soul's unfolding. As I adjusted, my priorities became clear: take care of my body through perimenopause and find guidance for my next steps. So, I hired a soul coach.

What I didn't expect was shamanic healing and initiation. One sunny spring morning, after a much-needed massage, my therapist handed me a flyer for an event called "The Shaman Tour: Condor Meets Eagle." The moment I touched the paper, a surge of energy whooshed up from my feet to my crown, leaving me reeling and breathless. I laughed out loud—"Whoa!"—but deep down, I knew it was a sign.

I attended the three-day retreat and found myself among healers, therapists, and two shamans from the Andes of Peru. It felt surreal, yet profoundly right. Over the following months, I received shamanic healings through ceremony and ritual, each one softening the grief and confusion I'd been carrying. My heart expanded, my shoulders relaxed, and I began to breathe more deeply. Nature became my teacher—trees, animals, and even the wind seemed to offer messages of love and guidance.

With my energy restored and optimism returning, I enrolled in graduate programs that built upon my honors degree in psychology. The journey became one of emotional healing and self-compassion. I stopped being so hard on myself and learned to accept my humanness. That self-acceptance led me to my next creation: *Soul Expressions*.

I asked the Universe to show me the way, envisioning myself as a soul healer and counselor with her own practice. And the Universe answered. Not long after graduating, I was invited to offer services at a local crystal shop and healing center. Saying *yes* to that opportunity affirmed everything I had learned about surrender and faith. For nearly a decade, I held private and group sessions, honing my counseling and teaching skills while helping others find their own soul expressions.

Looking back, I can see that even though I left corporate change management, I now facilitate something similar—change management for the soul. My focus is on helping women navigate midlife transitions, just as I did. Through surrender and trust, life continues to meet me halfway with synchronicities, Divine nudges, and guidance from the natural world. Birds, animals, and signs from nature still arrive like old friends with timely messages.

That first inner earthquake so many years ago was the beginning of my awakening. Through all the twists and transformations, I've learned to flow with life's blessings and heartaches. I've become grounded, resilient, and able to meet change with grace.

And now, I sleep well, I love deeply, and I live what I call my *soul expression*—a life led by trust, authenticity, and the quiet wisdom of the whispers within.

Reflection

1. Have you ever found yourself committed to something in your life that no longer fits—such as a relationship, a job, a role, or even a living space? What did you do when you realized it no longer aligned with who you were becoming?

2. Have you ever faced a confusing or uncertain time and asked the Universe, God, or Source for guidance? What happened when you asked? Did seeking guidance help bring clarity or peace?

3. Do you trust and act on your intuition? If yes, how has following your intuition supported you? If not, how can you open to exploring and developing a deeper relationship with it?

She Became the Fire

Truth-telling. Bold steps. Fear met with courage.

Once the spark is claimed, there comes a moment when hesitation falls away, and a woman moves from knowing to *being*. I remember seasons when fear still whispered, but it no longer led. Truth did. I said *yes* to paths that once felt impossible and no to what drained my spirit—even when my voice trembled. That was the moment I became the fire.

This chapter is about embodied action. These are stories of women who stopped waiting for permission and began living from their inner authority. They spoke truths long held inside. They took brave leaps—reinventing careers, leaving familiar places, reclaiming their power. Fear was present, but courage was stronger. Lit from within, these women stepped into the world with clarity, conviction, and trust. This is not the end of the journey—it is the season of becoming.

The Reclaimed Woman

ELAINE C. TORRANCE-GINGRICH

There was a time when I was a stranger in my own skin.

I wore the masks so well that even I forgot who lived beneath them. I gave away my "yes" when my soul was screaming "no." I was the "understanding one," the one who didn't make waves. I silenced my truth so I could be chosen, loved, and accepted, until the silence was louder than my own heartbeat.

For a long time, I thought that was a strength. I thought survival meant shrinking. I thought being loved meant abandoning myself.

But when you deny your truth long enough, life will burn it down for you.

When the fire came, I believed I had been destroyed. I didn't know then that I was standing in the ashes of everything I wasn't.

Reclamation is born there, in the fire! It was in the stillness of my undoing that I first heard the faint whisper: "Come home to yourself."

I will never forget the day I lost my first husband.

The hospital called and said he had taken a turn overnight, and I needed to get there. The sound of my sobs echoed in a room that suddenly felt too big, too empty, too cruel. I screamed at the doctor, "What did you do to my husband?" My hands shook as my whole body refused to accept the words, "He is brain dead, and it's just a matter of time before his body follows. Here's the DNR to sign if you don't want us taking any extreme measures."

I was forced to make a decision I wasn't prepared to make. My husband's body began to seize, and they all stood around, waiting for me to tell them what to do. That's when I heard the whisper in my ear, "I am no longer there." An eerie calm came over me as I intuitively knew that was my husband speaking to me, which gave me the courage to sign the DNR. I watched as he took his last breath. The image of my daughter shaking her father's foot, screaming, "Daddy, wake up," is forever burned in my heart. My world tilted. It didn't just stop; it collapsed.

Grief consumed everything. The silence of his absence roared through the house. I went through the motions of daily life, but inside I was scattered, fragmented, unrecognizable even to myself.

On the outside, I kept performing, showing up as the strong one for my girls, the one who could hold it all together. But inside, every breath hurt. Every laugh felt stolen. Every smile a betrayal.

I thought the loss had destroyed me. I thought I would never rise again.

But grief had a way of stripping me bare. And in the hollow ache of loss, a question flickered: *Who am I now?*

The first spark didn't come as light. It came in the years that followed my husband's passing. I had remarried. We moved out of state. My mother passed away. My sister-in-law passed away. My late husband's parents both passed. Loss and grief became all too familiar staples in my life and the lives of my daughters. Grief stripped me bare.

And yet, in the hollow ache of loss, something stirred. One calm evening, while on vacation by the ocean, with the full moon clear in the sky, my chest began to burn. My hands trembled. My whole body felt like it was waking up from a long sleep. A whisper rose, trembling but undeniable: No more.

No more betraying myself to be loved. No more silencing my

truth to keep the peace. No more abandoning my body, my voice, my soul.

The whisper wasn't dramatic. It wasn't loud. It was a quiet, full-bodied, "No more." That moment of defiance—born not of anger but of deep, lived grief—became the seed of reclamation.

Reclamation was not neat and tidy. It did not come with polite and pretty bows. It came with rage. With grief. With tears that burned down my cheeks like holy water. I raged at the years I had given away. At the girl inside me who had been told she was too much, not enough, unworthy. At the woman who had swallowed her voice so often that she forgot its sound.

And then I held her—all the previous versions of myself. I let her weep. I told her she never had to abandon herself again. Reclamation was remembering all the parts of me I had buried: the wild woman who spoke without apology. The soft woman who felt deeply without shame. The sovereign woman who knew her worth was not negotiable.

I started to write again. I began to dance again. I let my body lead instead of punishing it for being alive. Every act of remembering felt like fire in my veins. I felt fierce, alive, unstoppable.

From the ashes, I rose—not as the woman I pretended to be, but as the one I had always been beneath the masks. This reclaimed woman is not perfect. Nor always polished. She does not have all the answers. But she is whole.

I no longer wait for permission to be myself or shrink to be loved. I no longer apologize for taking up space. I speak my truth, even when my voice shakes. I honor my body as sacred ground. I love from overflow, not from self-abandonment.

Reclamation wasn't about becoming new but rather remembering who I was before the world told me who to be.

And that is who I am now. Now, when I walk into a room, I no longer wonder if I belong because I belong to myself. When I share my story, I no longer fear judgment. My story is my power.

When I love, I no longer bleed myself dry. I love from a place of wholeness, of sovereignty, of choice. I am not the woman I once was. I am the woman I was always meant to be. This is ME!

For so long, I believed I was broken, that I had failed, that it was too late. But I see now: I was never broken, never too late—I was being remade.

I once thought the fire came to destroy me. I know now it came to free me. While the details of my journey are uniquely mine, this truth is universal: We are never as lost as we think. Even in the darkest embers, the whisper of reclamation waits.

I rose. I found the pieces I thought I'd lost. I remembered the sound of my own voice. And when I did, I discovered something sacred: My wings were never given to me.

They were waiting in the ashes, all along.

Reflection

1. Where have I abandoned myself to be loved, accepted, or safe, and what truth is asking to be reclaimed now?

2. If I declared "no more" today, what patterns, stories, or masks would I burn away in the fire of reclamation?

3. Who is the woman I am becoming when I choose myself fully, in my voice, my body, my boundaries, and my truth? Describe her. Call her forward.

Choosing the Warrior Path of Peace

ENGRACIA GILL

I never taught anything without passing on my own lessons. I grew up in the Democratic Republic of the Congo, in the heart of Africa. Life threw me many hard knocks, even as a little girl. I survived war and family turbulence. Fortunately, early on, I discovered the great wisdom paths of Buddhism and Taoism and many more. Those paths helped me deeply. One time that I will never forget, I rose from a devastating encounter with my father into wisdom and peace.

My husband, Mike, and I were out biking. I had borrowed his friend's bike. We had risen early, and the air was soft, the fields bathed in a golden sunlight. I was so awed by the beauty of the day that I neglected my riding. Suddenly, we took a right turn onto a newly paved road. My bike sped toward my husband's back wheel. Out of control, I hit his back tire. I slid onto the side of the road, planting my face and filling my mouth with gravel. *"Oh my God,"* I groaned, *"I've broken all my teeth!"* Though my teeth were intact, my mouth was cut inside and out and I needed stitches.

My flesh mended. My heart did not. Weeks before, I had gone

to work at a retreat in England. I was a budding psychotherapist, teaching women to find acceptance. I decided to hop home to Brussels and leave Eliana, my vivacious daughter, with my parents. We arrived on a perfect April morning. Mom greeted us with joy. I stayed long enough to ensure Eliana got acclimated and hear about their plans. Dad was taking her to a professional soccer game. Eliana loved soccer passionately. A real professional soccer game would be a treat. In my mind, she was set.

I plunged into my work across the pond. One evening, I touched base with Eliana. Her tone had lost its peppy timber. After the soccer game, she confessed, Grandpapa was mad at her. He forbade her to call her dad. My heart dropped. Eliana's dread ate at my heart. "You have done nothing wrong, sweetheart. Daddy will call you instead. Honey, I know you are strong; give your fear to God. It will not change Grandpapa; it will give you courage." I tried to sound more confident than I felt. Mike called Eliana as often as possible.

Time crawled on, my heart hurting for my daughter. Finally, the retreat ended. Up at the crack of dawn, I grabbed the first taxi out to catch the plane back to my precious angel. Traffic clogged up all the arteries to Heathrow. I arrived with barely minutes to make my flight! *"I will not miss this flight!"* I prayed incessantly through the gates and the throngs of people, elbowing my way to my gate. I arrived at the gate, the last one on the plane!

In my seat, relief soon morphed to angst. Dad's contorted, angry face kept popping up. So many memories crowded in with his rages … then in floated the memory of another airport in Dacca, Bangladesh. Dad's rage had detonated in public at the airport. At the baggage carousel, Dad's blazing eyes obliterated my mother. Soon after I embraced them both, Dad started hurling insults at Mom in a booming voice that stopped people in their tracks.

I froze. "Dad," I said in a firm voice, "if you do not stop right this instant, I am taking the first plane back to Texas."

Dad saw my resolve. He stopped.

Hmm, another airport, another confrontation, I thought.

The loudspeaker jolted me back into the present. We were landing in Brussels. I vowed to face Dad calmly. The mother tigress in me was ready. All I would say was, "Your rage is no longer acceptable."

I spotted Dad at the luggage carousel, his rumpled trench coat hung on his shoulders, his face set in cold fury. I uttered some greeting, "Thank you for picking me up." Dad's smile was forced. We walked to the parking garage. Alone, waiting for the elevator, Dad pounced. The ominous moment had arrived.

"Eliana is an impossible child. She has been unhappy with everything. All she does is retreat to her room! She is rude, impolite, and spoiled," he shouted. I answered. "No, Dad, you are the adult. Your unreasonable expectations are the problem."

We stepped into the elevator. I returned every insult with firmness. The elevator halted, and a stranger stepped in. As soon as the stranger left, Dad resumed his shouting. Then Dad darted out of the elevator. Outside the elevator, he stopped, confused. He babbled, "I can't find the car ..." He was stumped, disoriented by his own rage. His eyes, haggard, kept darting around.

Relief flooded me. His virulent temper dissolved like sugar in water. Finally, we pulled up at the flat, and Eliana was in my arms. Mom watched with tears in her eyes. Dad marched past. He sat in his chair, the newspaper his barricade. "*Schatje* (darling)," Mom whispered.

"Don't worry, Mom. I'm here now," I whispered back. "We're going to grab a bite out."

"Mom, Grandmaman took me to the mall for every meal! It got so boring!" Eliana confessed to me while walking.

"Grandmaman did not cook the whole time you stayed with them?" I asked, incredulous. "Wow, that is not the mom I know. I'm sorry, sweetheart ..." my voice trailed. Eliana hugged me tighter. I knew of Mom's struggles with her memory. I had been the one to take her to her assessment. I suspected her repeated questions were early signs of dementia. *Mom's dementia has progressed rapidly. I now see the strain Dad is under.*

We rose early to catch our morning flight. "I'm leaving a hundred dollars to cover to cover calls to Mike, Dad."

"That's not necessary," he answered.

I hugged Mom with a heavy heart. I said goodbye to Dad. He did not hug me.

Once home, life drew me out into all that I loved. But my heart stayed closed. In meditation, a dark cloud hovered over thoughts of Dad. I wanted peace but I was stuck.

Dad's emotional assault had left a foul taste in my mouth. One morning, in the shower, I clearly saw the link between Dad's emotional assault and the biking accident. Dad's abuse hung around my heart and the accident externalized its toxicity so I could expel it. Dad had wished to muzzle my voice, to no avail. The biking fall was a call to attention.

I needed to transform the foul taste of bitterness. I urgently needed a way to peace. I turned to Thich Nhat Hanh, a Buddhist monk known for his wisdom. He taught that writing a gratitude letter could create a bridge of peace. I had so much bitterness, so little gratitude. Warmed by its promise, however, I composed the letter.

Writing the letter proved exceptionally painful. Yet I persisted. Memories of Dad emerged: him sharing poetry and art with me, our vivid intellectual discussions on many subjects. I had felt seen by him then. I took the plunge. I sent the letter. My mouth healed and so did my heart.

Dad never mentioned the letter. "Dad, I sent you a letter a few months ago. Did you receive it?" I asked one day.

"Yes, I did," he stated.

I felt a metamorphosis. Now I spoke with peace and strength. When Dad got angry at me, I breathed affirmations repeatedly— a "peace warrior" from the inside out.

When Mom died, Dad's tenderness toward me grew. Soon loving kindness and peace blossomed. Dad shared cherished memories of his life with Mom. He started his letters with "Engracia, *ma cherie* (my darling)." He always greeted me with those words on the phone. "Engracia, *ma cherie*" were the words I ached to hear after his death.

Speaking my truth required strength. Transforming bitterness into peace required courage. The biking fall was the hard knock life threw at me to dig deep. Growth often comes with hard knocks. When they come, I focus on the lesson to get me through the pain. A Buddhist precept is to accept that pain is inevitable, suffering is not. Focusing on the lesson and the growth halted unnecessary suffering.

1. Where in your life are you being invited to transform bitterness or hurt into something more spacious—like understanding, compassion, or peace?

2. How do old family patterns still influence your reactions today, and what truth are you finally ready to speak with clarity and strength?

3. What "hard knock" in your life might be calling you to look deeper—to find the lesson beneath the pain and rise with greater wisdom?

Becoming the Whisper

LISA HROMADA

There was always a whisper. Long before I ever knew what it meant. Long before my life purpose predictions were shared. Before I ever read the many nightly sessions—channeled by my dad and handwritten by my mom—tucked away in her bedroom closet.

I felt it. A Divine presence. I felt it in my childhood room, coloring on my bed, nestled among pink pillows and a circle of stuffed animals. I felt it as I ran down the hallways of our home, sensing a presence I couldn't explain. I felt it in the haze of night wakings, stirred by Divine visions I didn't yet understand.

I knew there was something ... different. A quiet knowing, like a secret between my soul and the Universe. It wasn't loud or dramatic—just a hum beneath the surface of everything. A whisper I couldn't explain but couldn't ignore.

As far back as I can remember, I have had spiritual experiences that feel like gentle truths rising through the veil. In dreams, loved ones visited after they passed. In journaling, wise words moved through my pen. Light danced across my room like silent messengers of love. I felt the presence of children and others in spirit—playful, joyful, tender. During one of my most challenging moments, an angelic woman appeared over me. And in quiet meditation, Love wrapped around me like a blanket and whispered, *You are not alone.*

For decades, my mom tried to write the book the loving souls and Wise Ones had asked for—the sacred messages trance-channeled through my dad when I was an infant. Night after night, they sat together on our brown tweed couch: my mom to his left, waiting patiently, my dad in meditation. Then suddenly, his head would fling back, his mouth opening with a sharp gasp. My mom was always taken aback in those moments, unsure what was truly happening.

Moments later, he would fall still—head lowered, eyes closed, body relaxed. That was when the souls and Wise Ones came through—full of eagerness, overflowing with Divine Love—ready to share their messages with the world, all for the purpose of writing a book on Divine Love and the human experience.

My mom carried both the weight of their love and the burden of their request. Many times, in my childhood, she confided how alone she felt, overwhelmed by the surreal nature of it all. As the years passed, she would call me in tears—heartbroken because she didn't know how to write the book. They were the same tears I remembered from childhood, when she told me how defeated she felt that the book still wasn't written. She was convinced she was failing them when all she longed to do was honor them.

It was hard watching her carry that weight. At night, I'd peek into her room and see her at her desk, back to me, typing on her old typewriter, doing her best to capture the sessions. Later, after I had grown and moved away, I could still recall the frustration in her voice—exhausted, worn down from trying.

Friends and family dismissed the channeling as nonsense. Some even called my dad unstable. Yet my mom never wavered. And neither did I.

Even as a young girl, I believed her—not only because I loved her, but because I felt the truth of it deep in my bones. I sensed there was more to this life, a deeper purpose for our being here. I was drawn to all things spiritual. I longed to understand what it meant to be a soul having a human experience. I was curious about my dreams, my intuitive nudges, the mysteries I couldn't explain.

So many times, I wanted to say, "Mom … I think it's me. I think I'm meant to write the book."

From my earliest memories, I carried the feeling that those sessions were meant for me—that I was here to do something meaningful with the hundreds of messages. But I didn't yet have the courage. I didn't want to take from her what she still hoped to complete.

And still, I knew.

The signs were always there—predictions, confirmations, and most of all that quiet, steady knowing.

On the surface, I lived a full life—college, work, marriage, motherhood.

And then one day, it all came together.

I was thirty-eight years old. My mom and I stood together in the kitchen of my rental home, leaning against the sink, talking the way mothers and daughters do. The late afternoon light spilled across the counter, warm and golden, while the faint hum of the refrigerator filled the pauses between our words. My newborn daughter slept nearby, wrapped in the hush of her dreams, and my young son sat at the dining table just beyond the counter, quietly absorbed in his show.

And then the air became still—the kind of quiet that feels like the world is holding its breath.

That's when she said it.

"Lisa," she began, "I've tried for years to write the book the souls and Wise Ones asked for. I just … can't. I don't believe I'm the one to write it. I feel like I've failed them." Her eyes brimmed with tears. "Can I give the sessions to you? Would you do something with them?"

I didn't hesitate. I'd known the answer all my life. "Yes," I said with a smile. "I will."

And the whisper inside me? It leaped. My heart swelled with indescribable joy and relief. At last, the whisper had found its voice. In that moment, something sacred passed between us—unspoken yet deeply felt. A torch was being passed—not only from mother to daughter, but from one soul's steward to another. The air felt lighter, as if the unseen world had exhaled. She could finally release what she had carried with such love, and I could finally receive what had always been mine to hold.

That moment in the kitchen cracked me open. Everything made sense—the dreams, the spiritual nudges, the inner ache, the childhood whispers. All of it had led to that single, Divine yes.

From the moment I accepted the sessions, the path unfolded with Divine ease. Within three months, I had written two manuscripts. Soon after, they were picked up by a publisher. By fall, they were in the hands of readers, and I began to speak about them.

I stepped into the very words channeled about me when I was a baby: "Lisa will carry the mantle of wisdom forward." "She is a spokesperson for the Creator." "She will bring forth leadership and direction to this new age."

And yet ... I was terrified. The first time I stood in front of a live audience, I could feel my heart pounding like a thousand drums in my chest.

You'd think that walking your soul's path would make it easier. But I had to face every shadow within me—fear of being judged, misunderstood, misquoted ... fear of being seen. I wasn't a trained speaker. I preferred the quiet corners, the places where I could contribute without attention.

But purpose doesn't ask for your comfort. It asks for your courage.

And the more I showed up, the more I realized—it wasn't just about writing a book. It wasn't even about me.

It was about the sacred work meant to move through me. About following soul nudges and saying yes without needing to see the whole path. About bringing light into the world, even when I felt afraid. About listening to the whisper that had always been there, reminding me: *It was always you, Lisa. You were the seed of love. You were the one.*

So here I am. A messenger. A mother. A woman who said yes.

And though the fear still visits me from time to time, it no longer leads. The whisper does.

That was my kitchen moment. I believe we all have one, waiting quietly for us. It might not come with fireworks or a sign in the sky. It might arrive softly—with sunlight on the counter, a baby asleep in the other room, a preschooler watching a show, and a mother offering a promise wrapped in love. And you say yes.

Because the path doesn't require certainty—only willingness. The whisper had always guided me. The wings were already mine—I had only to remember them, claim them as my own, and rise.

And so, I did.

Reflection

1. What quiet "whisper" or inner knowing has been with you for years—and how might your life change if you finally said yes to it?

2. Where in your life are you being invited to carry forward a legacy—family, spiritual, or ancestral—that feels both sacred and uniquely yours?

3. What fears arise when you step toward your purpose, and how might you show up with courage anyway?

Becoming Enough

JORDAN GUADALUPE

It all began in first grade. We were learning to read, and my teacher, Mrs. K., had a different student read aloud to the class each week. That week, it was my turn.

I had chosen my book days earlier, practicing it over and over until I could practically recite it in my sleep. I was proud of how prepared I was, and as I walked to the front of the classroom, my little body buzzed with excitement. Twenty pairs of eyes followed me to the chair beside Mrs. K. I opened the book, smoothed the page, and read with confidence. Every word rolled out easily, and I was sure she'd be impressed.

When I finished, I looked up at her, expecting a smile, maybe even some praise I could share with my parents. Instead, her face was stern. She reached for another book and handed it to me. "Here, read this one now." Panic rose instantly. My heart raced. I wasn't ready for this. With a shaky voice, I stumbled through the first line, tripping over the words. The silence in the room pressed down on me as my classmates stared. My cheeks burned hot.

Finally, Mrs. K. stopped me. "Back to your seat. You need more practice," she said loud enough for everyone to hear. Humiliation washed over me. I had only tried to do what was asked.

Why would she put me on the spot like that? I walked back to my desk with my head down and my heart bruised.

That moment planted a seed of shame that would take root and grow. Through elementary school, I struggled to keep up. Teachers sent notes home, voicing concerns. By fourth grade, one even suggested I repeat the year. Every assignment felt like proof that I wasn't enough. I constantly compared myself to my classmates, always coming up short. So I adapted. I learned to play small. To disappear into the back of the classroom, avoid raising my hand, and never risk being exposed again. My only goal became to stay unnoticed, be average, and survive without drawing attention.

By high school, I discovered something that seemed to solve everything: alcohol. I don't remember my very first drink, but I remember the first time I realized what it could do for me. I was with friends, laughing and talking about a party the night before. My head throbbed from the hangover, but my heart felt light. For the first time in years, I had been carefree, relaxed, and bold. "I love alcohol," I thought. "When I drink, I can finally be me." It was intoxicating not just in the literal sense but in how it silenced the anxious voice that had run my life since childhood. And if drinking made me likable, confident, and free—why wouldn't I embrace it?

And so I did. Through my late teens and into my twenties, I built an identity around being the fun, rebellious party girl. My nights were spent in bars and clubs; my mornings, in hangovers and regret. Outwardly, I looked like I was having the time of my life. Inwardly, I knew it was a mask that hid my shame, insecurity, and the little girl who never felt enough.

By my late twenties, the cracks began to show. Each night out felt emptier than the last. I carried guilt and shame like a heavy load on my back. I could no longer ignore the restlessness gnawing at me. Something deep inside whispered that I was meant for more, that I was better than this cycle of parties and payback.

By thirty, that whisper became a roar. I felt like I was crawling out of my own skin. One morning after a long night of partying, I looked in the mirror and didn't recognize myself. My eyes looked vacant, hollow. The reflection staring back was a stranger. I thought, "Is this really all there is?"

I longed for purpose, impact, and a chance to see what I was made of. I remembered discovering the law of attraction in my early twenties and how it had once filled me with joy and possibility. But even then, something was missing. I didn't love myself enough to step into my potential truly. And deep down, I knew exactly what was holding me back: my lifestyle.

Letting it go felt terrifying. Alcohol had been my crutch, my identity, and my way of belonging. But the truth was clear: staying the same had become more painful than changing. And so, with resolve, I quit.

Not long after, a catalog arrived in the mail from a local retreat center. Flipping through the glossy pages, one headline stopped me cold: *Find Your Calling*. My heart pounded. "This is it," I thought. "This is what I've been searching for." I registered on the spot. My hands shook as I entered my payment information, a rush of excitement and fear coursing through me. Quitting alcohol and signing up for the retreat felt like two halves of the same leap. I wasn't just removing something toxic from my life—I was making space for something sacred to emerge.

But that space was uncomfortable. Without alcohol clouding my vision, I realized I barely knew who I was. Who was I without the party-girl persona? Without the same circle of friends? Without the false confidence drinking had given me? The loneliness was crushing. Friday nights, once filled with plans, now stretched out empty. Friends drifted away or didn't understand the new version of me. In social situations, I felt exposed again, just like that little girl in the classroom. Everyone else sipped cocktails and laughed easily, while I sat quietly in my own head.

But I refused to give up. Each time I pushed myself outside my comfort zone—attending a gathering while sober, setting a boundary, starting a business—I built strength. Every challenge conquered became part of the foundation of a new identity.

One of the most pivotal moments came after my career transition into coaching, when I was invited to speak at a women's conference. On the surface, I was thrilled by an opportunity to share my message. But beneath the excitement was panic. Public speaking had always been one of my greatest fears.

As I waited to hear my introduction from the MC, I could barely breathe. My heart pounded the same way it had in first grade when Mrs. K. handed me that unexpected book. But this time, I whispered to myself, *"I'm not running."* I walked on stage, accepted the mic, and began to speak. As the words flowed, the fear melted. I realized that fear's only real power is in the anticipation. Once you step into it, it loses its grip. That moment changed me. It proved that I could face anything.

Meanwhile, I had been reconnecting with the parts of myself I had buried. I rediscovered old passions and uncovered new strengths. The qualities I once tried to numb—sensitivity, depth, whimsy—I came to see as my gifts. I wasn't broken; I was resilient. I wasn't stupid; I simply processed differently. I wasn't inadequate; I was enough.

Most of all, I realized I could choose how I felt in any moment, and that choice created my reality. The law of attraction became not just a theory but a way of living. And with that awareness came my calling: to coach, teach, and guide others to emerge out of the shadows of shame and fear, just as I had done.

Looking back, I see the thread that runs through it all. The little girl who shrank in her chair, the teenager who drowned her voice in alcohol, the woman who stared into the mirror and saw no one looking back—she was never lost. She was emerging. Every moment of shame, every stumble, every heartbreak was the soil that grew my new identity. The pain wasn't wasted. It was the teacher who led me here.

Today, I no longer sit in the back of the room. I stand on stages.

I speak my truth. I live in alignment with who I am. Fear hasn't faded away completely, but it no longer stops me from saying *yes* to the beautiful opportunities that present themselves to me. And my purpose is clear: to help others see that their struggles are not their end—they are the beginning. Because when you find the courage to face yourself—the fear, the shame, the loneliness—you discover the truth: you were never broken. You were always becoming.

1. Think about the parts of yourself you hide to feel accepted. What mask do you wear, and what would it feel like to slowly remove it?

2. Recall a time when you felt "not enough." What beliefs did that moment plant in you, and how might you begin to rewrite them today?

3. Is there an area of your life where staying the same has become more painful than changing? What's one small step you can take toward the version of yourself you long to become?

Just like a Firefly

RUTHIE LEWIS

How could I have known that chasing fireflies would be the spark that reclaimed my soul?

I'm no longer that barefoot little girl running through her grandparents' backyard, chasing fireflies as though she glowed herself. Back then, my soul's light shone its brightest. I was wild and free, unaware of how easily a light can dim.

He was my first love, and when he looked at me, butterflies filled my stomach. I adored his Beatles-style hair and broad shoulders, symbols of strength I mistook for safety. On our first date, though, something felt off. He barely acknowledged me, letting the door swing shut in my face. My "good girl" conditioning told me to smile and pretend it didn't happen. Red flags kept waving, but I painted each one the color of love—or maybe approval. I wanted to be what I thought I *should* be, not what my soul whispered I already was.

When the minister said, "I pronounce you man and wife," I believed I was stepping into happily ever after. I didn't realize I was walking into a gamble for my very being. My purpose became to love no matter what, to be the perfect wife and mother. Love never fails, right?

In our second apartment, I unpacked endless boxes, determined to make a cozy nest, though I hadn't chosen the job, the apartment, or even the city. My sapphire ring snagged on a box flap, and I drifted back to that picnic at Pikes Peak when he'd given it to me.

"The ring matches your sapphire eyes," he'd said.

I'd picked wildflowers that day and pressed them between the pages of a book to remember. When I found them again years later, brittle and faded inside *The Total Woman*, I felt like a fraud. I wasn't that woman—not even close.

One evening, I was driving home after a long day at work in his Camaro, borrowed because my own car was on its last legs. Then came the screech of tires, the crush of metal, the shattering of glass. My first thought wasn't pain—it was dread. *He's going to be so mad.* When I finally reached him by pay phone, his first words were, "How's my car?" My knees gave way. The injury wasn't physical; it was the death of something sacred inside me.

I kept pretending everything was fine, painting over my truth with "have-to" and "supposed-to," layering lies so thick I could barely breathe. I told myself the familiar clichés—*I'll just love harder, I'll try more*—while my light flickered lower and lower.

Then came the call: "Ruthie, this is Dr. Sanger's office. You're definitely pregnant!"

Hot tears ran down my face. Life pulsed through me, and I thought, *This will fix everything.* When I held our son, tiny and perfect, I believed love could rewrite our story. But cracks widened into canyons.

When our baby cried, he asked, "Why is he crying?"

I could only whisper, "That's what babies do." I was exhausted, unseen, and disappearing.

Years later, I sat at the dinner table with our two small children.

"Where's Daddy?" they asked.

The hole in my heart was as vast as the Grand Canyon. Pregnant again, I felt trapped and shrinking. My anger finally broke through the numbness: *This is not normal. How did I get here?*

One afternoon, while running errands, I realized I hadn't even smiled at the cashier. Once my default expression, joy, had vanished. I was existing, not living, my life force drained. I stepped outside and looked up at the sky, breathing deeply for what felt like the first time in years. Somewhere inside, I sensed a lighthouse flickering across the water, faint but steady. My soul whispered, *The journey begins.*

That night on the patio, memory found me. I could smell the grass, hear the laughter, and see the glow of fireflies dancing through twilight. In my mind, I chased them again, gathered them gently into a jar, delighting in their tiny sparks. But when their light began to fade, I unscrewed the lid. "You're free," I whispered, watching them rise into the darkening sky. One lingered, circling as if to say, *The lid is off,* before flying away. I realized I had lived most of my adult life inside a jar of my own making—its lid long gone, but my belief in limitation kept me trapped.

My silence and compliance had never been virtues. They were cages. I could no longer measure my choices by how they aligned with *his* needs. My heart ached for my children, but I knew that staying dimmed in that jar would destroy us all. I called a friend, voice trembling. "I know what I have to do," I said. "I'm flying free."

Freedom wasn't easy. Boundaries were ignored, gaslighting and judgment followed, friends drifted away, and my children's hearts were confused. But peace called louder than fear. Each step toward my light brought me closer to shore. I devoured books, noticed synchronicities, and listened to teachers who spoke directly to my soul. One day, a speaker looked straight at me and asked, "What are you waiting for permission to do?"

That's when writing found me again. A workshop invitation appeared as if by magic. I didn't have the money, but I trusted the call—and the funds showed up, too. I began to write furiously—blogs, essays, and eventually my novel *Fireflies.* My passion reignited,

I became a life coach, determined to tell every woman still trapped, "The lid is off!"

Then, just as my children and I began to feel steady again, tragedy struck. My son found his father's body—he had taken his own life with the rifle they once used together. Grief swept in like a tidal wave, and guilt whispered its venom: *You broke the family. You caused this.*

But even through the pain, I refused to let the darkness consume me. I had worked too hard to reclaim my light. I journaled every day, anchoring myself in truth, remembering the courage it took to leave, and honoring the light that refused to die. Heartbreak was real, but so was my birthright—joy, abundance, freedom.

Now, when I look up at the night sky, I see the same glow I once chased barefoot through summer grass. Fireflies flicker around me, whispering reminders: *You are free. The lid is off.* My story is no longer about survival—it's about becoming. And when I see other women standing in their own darkness, I want to tell them what I finally learned: Your light was never lost. It was only waiting to be remembered.

Stand back and watch the light show.

Reflection

1. When have you dimmed your own light, and what would it look like to let it shine again?

2. What does freedom feel like in your body, and where can you welcome more of it into your life?

3. What story about yourself are you ready to rewrite into something truer and more empowering?

Wings Remembered

Integration. Flight. Soul-led living.

Beautiful soul, rising is not the end of the journey—it is the beginning of a new way of being. I know this season well, where healing softens into integration and life begins to reflect the truth you've reclaimed. It's the moment when choices feel aligned, peace replaces striving, and you no longer question your worth or direction. You simply *live it*.

This chapter holds stories of women who did more than survive or heal—they soared. Their transformation came full circle, woven into how they love, lead, create, and move through the world. Here, intuition guides decisions, purpose fuels action, and freedom is lived from the inside out. These women have not only remembered their wings—they trust them. This is embodied flight. This is the remembering of who they have always been.

Wounds to Wings: Journey to Compassion and Forgiveness

JESSICA BANE ROBERT

I found my mother sitting on the edge of the tub, combing her hair down over her face. "What's the matter?" I asked. She remained motionless. "Let me see," I urged.

She parted her hair to reveal a deep gash across her forehead.

It was Christmas morning. My two children, then six and three, waited anxiously by the fire to open stockings.

But instead of the storybook Maine Christmas my mother had promised, I was leaving my children behind to drive through spitting snow to the emergency room. She had fallen on the ice in the frigid dark. She wasn't sure if she'd blacked out. She could have frozen to death just outside the door.

When we returned, my father looked at her with disdain and mocked her, calling her *turban head*, as he glared at the gauze bandages cocooning her skull.

Sadie and Jake watched the theater that I had grown accustomed to, their eyes darting first to grandmother, then to grandfather. Seeing the confusion and disappointment on my children's faces stirred a sickening muck of memories and emotions in my gut. I saw the pain of my childhood clearly through their eyes. The scene, all too familiar; joy eclipsed by my parents' drama and chaos.

Christmas cut short, we packed up and headed for Massachusetts. In the car, I finally exhaled. I held my breath in the presence of my parents—my breath, my words, my hopes.

As the snowy highway unfolded, I hid my face from the kids and stifled tears while visions of my childhood anguish flashed on the screen of my mind like road signs passing by. *She could have frozen to death out there. How many more falls would it take? And my father, merciless. Luke would never treat me that way.*

I vowed then that my children would not inherit my pain. But demons lurking beneath my cool facade would have to be faced.

Just once, in college, I tried therapy. In a dusty campus office, I unloaded everything—the heap of secrets, the ache of years. The psychologist looked at me and said, "How have you managed? I would have thrown myself off a bridge."

It landed like a suggestion, not compassion. I left feeling broken, hopeless, alone—the way I felt leaving my parents that Christmas morning when I had vowed to heal my wounds to be the best partner and parent I could. But how?

I would attempt healing the way my hyper-independent self had always done things—alone. Night after night, I sat in our den, a stack of psychology and self-help books by my side, studying children of alcoholics and codependent families.

The research was bleak. One alcoholic parent was bad, two worse. An *only* child of two alcoholic, co-dependent parents, forget it. There was little hope of developing self-esteem or forming healthy relationships. Statistics indicated that I was destined to be depressed, suicidal, or addicted myself. The vow I had made to my children kept me afloat, while the current of despair pulled me fast toward the very patterns I longed to escape.

Sometimes things must totally disintegrate before they can be rebuilt. As I sat each night reading and weeping, I began to drink—first a glass, then a bottle of wine. Perhaps I thought,

Can't beat them, join them. Or maybe, I foolishly wished that my self-destruction would get their attention or hurt them.

For months, I floated adrift on victimhood and suffering until Luke materialized before me with pleading eyes to break the spell. "What are you doing? This needs to stop." That night, a voice inside spoke, *This moment provides a new beginning. Jess, just begin again.*

What I know now—but didn't then—is this: when you surrender and kneel before the Universe to declare that you are ready to break patterns, ready to heal, the Universe conspires to meet you and provide what you need.

Like a damselfly, I had spent years holding my breath in the silt and mud. But I was about to learn that I could grow wings for the sky.

My first job out of college was as a liaison between the local high school and a homeless shelter. The students I supported had endured adversity *far* beyond mine. Yet my wounds allowed me to sit with theirs. They saw in my eyes that I knew something of their hurt, and I reflected back love and worthiness. As I encouraged their voices, my own wounds began to scab over. I learned to speak to myself the way I spoke to them. Teaching and mentoring became medicine.

Then came a reunification with my Uncle Teddy, an alcoholic himself, in recovery. He invited me to his home and asked, "What do you most want for yourself?" It was the first time anyone had asked me, or taught me to ask, this question.

I remember staring at the patio, my chest and throat tight, embarrassed and unable to answer. His offer would be generous, and I felt unworthy. But when I looked up at Teddy, someone who knew much of my history, his eyes coaxed with love, and somehow, I listened to a feeling of longing and wiser knowing within. Teddy offered an important lesson—ask and be open to receiving. So, I asked for something big. Teddy paid for my MFA in Creative Writing.

The master's program rekindled a lifeline from childhood—writing. Growing up off the grid, isolated in the Maine woods, I had once turned to words to make sense of my inner and outer worlds. E. M. Forster's quote rang true: "How do I know what I think, until I see what I say?" Writing provided a voice, clarity, and catharsis. The practice helped make meaning of my life—and I would do it again.

My mentor, author Baron Wormser, encouraged me to write my story, and to write it whole—to see my parents in their complexity, to let the fullness of my life in, by holding pain and beauty side by side. Through facing and reliving all experiences on the page like exposure therapy, my scars softened, meaning surfaced. Writing taught me compassion—for those who had caused me pain as well as for myself.

When Teddy passed too soon, the wake of his absence revealed more gifts. His widow led me to a week-long healing retreat that changed everything. Sitting in a circle with other beautiful souls, we visualized, journaled, played—we cried, we laughed. For the first time, I was not alone on my journey. *I am that I am*, we chanted together, and the shame I carried dissolved. I felt the light of the Divine, of the Creator, of my connections to all others grow inside me, providing a salve for all the wounded places within. In this circle, we reconnected with our inherent worth, realizing that we were more than our worst deeds, more than our painful stories. Forgiveness and a wholeness I had never known before became real.

Leaving taller, lighter, and able to look myself in the eye with love, I shed survival mode, and for the first time, felt free to dream. And dreams, I realized, could also be an inheritance.

So, I knelt before the Universe once more. What came next was a home that would become the Barred Owl Retreat—a sacred space where folks could gather to explore self-expression, self-discovery, and healing. The retreat manifested as a culmination of all that had come before in my life.

Unequivocally, I now know this: All experience—the beautiful and the breaking—weaves into one breeze that carries us to our fullest expression. Pain teaches us, shapes us, and allows us to know its flipside—the updraft that is JOY.

Although my parents caused me deep hurt, I learned to see them as myself, in all their fullness: their journey, their intelligence, warmth, and resourcefulness. Gifts I carry because of them.

When I dared to embrace the whole of my life, especially the parts that almost undid me, I transformed. Each painful experience helped me rise, again and again, toward a higher, wiser self—each trial part of a Divine curriculum, a sacred unfolding.

We grow wings. We remember that we were made for flight all along.

Reflection

1. Write about a time when sorrow and joy lived side by side in your life. What did that tension teach you about compassion—for yourself and for others?

2. What painful patterns or beliefs have you inherited, and how are you choosing to break cycles for yourself or the next generation?

3. When you look back on your life, what moments felt like your undoing, yet later revealed themselves as part of your sacred life's curriculum? How might you reframe one current challenge in your unfolding?

Listening to the Voice Within

BETH MYERS

As I wound my way down that familiar, twisting road on a dark, chilly night in October 1985, I could feel the weight of despair pressing on me with no hope of shaking this feeling. Gripping the wheel with white-knuckled fear and erratic thoughts of what I intended to do to deal with my perceived inadequacies, I fought back tears. My mission was to find the perfect rendezvous with the splintering of a telephone pole to relieve the huge waves of anxiety that were crashing down on me.

Suddenly, a voice thundered through my mind—firm, clear, unmistakable: "Go to your parents."

I listened. Trembling and sobbing, I turned the car toward safety.

As I drove to my parents' home, my mind replayed the moment it all began to crumble—my very first day of teaching. I stood before the class, holding a teddy bear meant to create connection and comfort. Instead, a student punched it in the stomach and shouted defiantly, "You can't tell me what to do!" The heat of humiliation surged through me as the other children stared, wide-eyed. I tried to steady myself, but something deep inside had already cracked.

I stood there, frozen in fear. My voice, barely more than a whisper, asked him repeatedly to sit down, but he didn't budge.

I had no idea what to do. Nothing in my student teaching had prepared me for this level of defiance. The most I'd ever encountered before was a child talking too much. This was different. This felt like danger—like a warning siren blaring inside me that I couldn't silence.

My heart pounded in my chest as I tried to stay calm for the rest of the class, but inside, I was unraveling. Mercifully, the schedule offered a reprieve. That transition helped shift the external energy, but inside, I was just trying to hold it together. I didn't tell a soul. I buried it. Stuffed it down. My shame was louder than my voice. I was afraid if I said it out loud, it would confirm what I already feared: Maybe I wasn't cut out for this.

Humiliation punctuated the end of my first day as my mom arrived with flowers and a balloon, ready to celebrate my "new beginning." The moment I saw her, I collapsed in tears. She thought she was walking into a proud milestone—what she found was the wreckage of my spirit. I was already drowning in self-doubt, and no one knew how close I was to breaking.

A little over sixty days into my first year of teaching, I was coming undone. Every morning, I arrived at school by 5:30 a.m., greeting the custodian with a nervous smile, clutching my lesson plans like armor—scurrying to gain control before the children arrived. And yet, by afternoon, my classroom would slip further from my grasp. What had once been my dream—standing among eager young minds—now felt like the slow death of my spirit.

Upon arriving in the dark of night, I rang the doorbell and collapsed into the safety of my parents' arms. Through gasping tears, I confessed what I had nearly done on the road. "I just … can't do it anymore," I whispered. The crushing pressure of responsibility, the ache of inadequacy, and the silent storm of depression had finally collided inside me. I felt like a failure. Lost. Unworthy. Out of control.

But instead of shame, they met me with unconditional love.

They held me close and told me what my heart needed most

to hear: "It's okay. If you need to walk away from teaching, we understand. We just want you safe." That night, I curled up in my childhood room, surrounded by echoes of innocence, and allowed myself to rest simply.

The next morning, my dad lay beside me on the bed, tears rolling silently down his cheeks. "Whatever you need to do, we're with you." His words cracked something open in me—just enough space to let the light back in.

My mom arranged an emergency appointment with her therapist. Sitting in that quiet office, I felt seen for the first time in what felt like forever. Her calm presence reminded me that I wasn't alone—and that there were still choices ahead. That conversation planted a sacred seed of healing.

She was the first of many guides on my path—hypnotherapists, cognitive behavioral therapists, expressive art and movement therapists, intuitive life coaches—all helping me piece together what had been buried under years of perfectionism and performance. Slowly, I began to reclaim myself. A journey of unlearning, remembering, and reimagining.

With trembling courage, I arranged a meeting with my principal. I fully intended to resign. Instead, he surprised me. "I believe you can be an excellent teacher," he said, meeting my eyes with sincerity. "Let us support you." He coordinated check-ins with the reading specialist, school support staff, and my grade-level team. What I expected to be the end of my teaching career became a new beginning.

My weekly sessions with my hypnotherapist became a lifeline. She helped me command control in my classroom with my voice and presence, not fear. She taught me to have compassion for myself, to acknowledge my emotions, and—just as importantly—to recognize the feelings of my students.

I enrolled in the school district's yearlong new teacher workshop and found camaraderie among others navigating the steep learning curve of first-year teaching. By spring, I was invited to return the following year and speak to incoming teachers about the power of seeking support. I was living proof that transformation was possible.

Back in my classroom, something shifted. My students could feel it. I began to trust myself—trust my ability to teach, to lead, to love. When I later found the same troubled boy who had punched my bear, banging his head against the floor, screaming, "I hate you! I hate my mother! I hate everyone!" I didn't flinch.

Instead of fear, I felt compassion. I remembered: *Hurt people hurt others.* And I added: *And they hurt themselves.*

That moment became my call. I didn't just want to teach. I wanted to help—truly help—children understand their own pain and how to move through it. I wanted to support teachers, too, and co-create safe, thriving classrooms. That summer, I enrolled in a master's program in school counseling. I needed to understand not just my students' behaviors—but my own.

The following year, a supervisor who had once marked me "Needs Improvement" visited my classroom and saw me joyfully leading my students in a learning game. "Wow," he said, smiling. "You're really growing into an effective teacher." I was. Because I was finally listening to the voice within me—not the critics, not the expectations, but my *true self.*

In the years that followed, I stepped into a series of roles that felt divinely timed. From teaching transitional first grade to supporting rural first grade students at a small country school, each step led me closer to my calling. Eventually, I was chosen as the founding school counselor for a brand-new elementary school. A sacred assignment to help build a community rooted in belonging, inclusion, and light. I remained there for sixteen magical years.

When I felt the call to spread my wings again, I declared what I needed: to be closer to home, serve fewer students, and have an office with a window. All three came to pass at the elementary school I went to as a child ... where I said I would never go.

I kept following the voice.

That same voice led me to become a certified law of attraction life coach and, later, to a portable, purpose-filled career supporting a transformational leader and coaching others on their path. I retired after thirty-one years in education and stepped fully into a flexible life of coaching, mentoring, and traveling the country with my wife, Kim, my soulmate and business partner.

Together, we've followed our long-held dream of full-time RV living. We've created a life of freedom and fulfillment—on our terms.

And now, as we journey across the country, we help others shine their light … especially in times of darkness.

Because healing begins when we get quiet enough to listen. To soften the shadows. To honor the inner wisdom. To trust the voice that rises from within. That voice didn't just save my life.

It gave me wings.

Reflection

1. Have you ever reached a breaking point that became a turning point? What wisdom did it reveal to you?

2. What is the "voice within" whispering to you right now? Are you allowing yourself the quiet to truly hear it?

3. If your soul could write one sentence for the next chapter of your life, what would it say?

The Healing Journey to My Joyful Yes

KELLEY GRIMES, MSW

I had been experiencing a firestorm of awakening that shook me to my core and illuminated my soul-inspired choices like a video timeline of my life. As outgrown roles and overwhelming responsibilities burned away, I found in the embers my truth, my light, and my soul's purpose reborn. This awakening untethered and profoundly unsettled me, as I was no longer bound to who I had been, yet my becoming still unfolded like a butterfly in a chrysalis. I felt the light pouring out in every direction of my life, reflecting both the radiance and shadows of my choices and the opportunities to heal and transform.

This powerful transformation had been building for some time, culminating in a tumultuous few months. The identities I had embraced for years suddenly felt uncomfortable, like clothing that no longer fit or expressed my true self. My soul had been telling me for years that there was more for me than the roles I played so well.

I had yearned to experience more creativity, spaciousness, and freedom. Recently, the roles in which I had become an expert drained my energy and inspiration. Instead of empowering me to grow, I felt my wings had been clipped. Since I was young, I had struggled with feeling overly responsible and had created a very full life—running my own business, working for two nonprofits, volunteering in the community, and dedicating much of my free time to my family and grandchildren while living in a four-generation household. I loved my life and was deeply grateful for my self-nurturing practices that allowed me to refill my well and joyfully engage in its sacred abundance.

Even with my commitment to self-nurturing, I began to feel I was living a life that no longer fit, as if there was little space for my soul's calling. My daily meditation practice revealed this unsettled yearning, reflected regularly in my journal entries. While in London, sitting in Hyde Park on a beautiful summer evening with my husband, Tony, and our cousin Paul, I declared that in the next few years I would change how I lived my life. Paul asked, "Why wait two years? Why not choose that life now?" As my identity of over-responsibility began to protest, my soul celebrated this new awakening.

When I returned home, I was invited to write a chapter for *The Power of Inner Sparkle*. In my chapter, "Radiate Your Inner Sparkle: The Sacred Art of Self-Nurturing," I wrote about the genesis of my life's work. It was powerful to acknowledge the challenges I had overcome and to honor the meaningful decisions I had made to cultivate a life filled with peace and joy. I was also able to witness how my feelings of responsibility and desire to keep everyone safe and cared for had reinforced my identity as a professional nurturer—a role I had begun to feel limited by.

A few days before the book launch party in Colorado Springs, called "Sparkle and Soar," Linda Joy asked me to participate in this book, *Embers to Wings*. Before answering, my eyes were drawn to a quote on my wall that I often read: "What if I fall? Oh, darling, what if you fly?" Saying a joyful yes to writing this chapter accelerated my transformation. On this trip to my birthplace, I began receiving many messages from winged creatures that reminded me to spread my wings and fly.

I was blessed to have my daughter Zoey and nine-month-old granddaughter Stella join me. After arriving at our Airbnb, we went to Whole Foods to purchase food for the weekend. As we got in the car, I noticed a bee on the windshield and quickly rolled up the windows so it wouldn't join us inside. The bee was at eye level and stayed with us the entire drive. I started talking to her and named her Beatriz, surprised she was able to stay on the windshield the whole trip. When we returned to the car, she was still there. I thought she must have a message for me and asked, "Beatriz, do you want to tell me something?" She turned toward me and began flapping her wings. I asked, "Are you telling me to fly?" Then she flew off.

I was moved to tears, feeling seen and affirmed by this inspiring message and blessing. My daughter and I acknowledged the Divine encouragement with awe and gratitude. We laughed through our tears, saying, "You can't make this shit up!" Later I learned that *Beatriz* means "bringer of joy and blessings."

I was overcome with emotion and gratitude for the Divine message I had received through that encounter. Over the weekend, I was blessed with many more magical winged encounters: dragonflies symbolizing change and enlightenment; butterflies symbolizing transformation and spiritual growth; birds symbolizing freedom, hope, and new beginnings; and even a bat symbolizing rebirth and transformation. I embraced these Divine blessings and the invitation to let go, release, and set myself free to take flight in my life. I also visited my childhood home, where I had a surprisingly magical experience reconnecting with my childhood self. I felt inspired, invigorated, and excited for what was to come next.

Then, right before leaving for the airport to fly home, my granddaughter started crying, held her breath, turned gray, and passed out in my daughter's arms. We thought she had died. After twenty long seconds, she began to regain consciousness, though she was lethargic and not very responsive. We called 911, and after the paramedics arrived and examined her, we learned that Stella had a breathing spell and would be okay.

My daughter and I were completely traumatized and still needed to get to the airport and fly home. On the drive, I began shaking and crying as the deep pain in my heart—the same pain that had motivated my over-responsibility for over a quarter of a century—erupted like a volcano in my chest. My nervous system was completely dysregulated, and the experience triggered old trauma, grief, and helplessness from being the primary caregiver for my daughter Fiona, who had epilepsy.

My grief crashed over me like a tsunami, and I was unable to work for two weeks. The shadows illuminated by my awakening heart and soul begged to be healed. I could see how these old feelings of helplessness and unsafety had led me to feel responsible for everyone's health, safety, and well-being—a trauma response. I began noticing how my strengths, leadership skills, and the many roles I had played in my life had been cultivated out of this trauma response. Healing these wounded parts of myself was essential for my soul's expanding journey, so I reached out to a trauma therapist, a shamanic healer, a nutritionist, and Mother Earth. I embraced all my self-nurturing practices that could ground and support me—meditating, walking at the beach, journaling, singing, praying, gardening, and massage.

Thank goodness for all the support I gathered, as the healing journey became extremely bumpy. Weeks of dizziness and vomiting led to losing nine pounds very quickly. I felt as if everything I needed to let go of to become who I was meant to be was being released from my body, and I experienced the storm of release like a volcano and an earthquake. It was very intense and surreal—and I was so grateful I survived.

I was able to heal, release the shadows, and honor the gifts of my trauma response, recognizing that some of my most in-

spiring qualities had grown out of those experiences. I let go of beliefs no longer serving me and returned home to myself, settling and integrating my nervous system like never before. From this grounded, integrated place in the home of my heart, I could authentically and enthusiastically connect with my joyful yes. My joyful yes reflected my soul's calling—not influenced by my trauma response, responsibilities, roles, or others' expectations. As a result, I stepped back from roles and responsibilities not rooted in my joyful yes and, like a butterfly, emerged from my chrysalis with space and freedom for my wings to unfurl and embrace my sacred soul's calling.

On this healing journey, I often listened to one of Alex Elle's guided meditations. I now understood why her closing words always moved me to tears: "One day I woke up singing a song I didn't know, saying a prayer I'd never prayed, holding seeds I'd never sown, yet the lyrics rolled off my lips like love, like my mother tongue, like the first language I'd ever known. And it was all so strange to choose myself yet again."

This sacred awakening of claiming my joyful yes was the rebirth of my soul.

Reflection

1. Where in your life have you outgrown an identity or role, and what truth is emerging beneath the ashes of what no longer fits?

2. What would it look like to listen more deeply to your own "joyful yes"—the soul-led guidance beneath obligation, fear, or over-responsibility?

3. Which old wounds or protective patterns are asking to be released so you can create more space, freedom, and breath for who you are becoming?

From Ashes to Amy

AMY LINDNER-LESSER

He died two days before my forty-third birthday. My kids were on their way home from camp, driven by two counselors, while I waited at the inn. Then the call came from the hospital: Steve's fight was over. One moment, I was a wife, a partner, a woman building a dream; the next, I was a widow, a single parent, and the sole owner of a twenty-room inn, trying to survive a life I hadn't chosen. Not exactly the birthday gift I wanted. My dreams were shattered. Suddenly, a voice thundered through my mind—firm, clear, unmistakable: "Go to your parents."

It wasn't a surprise—he had terminal cancer—yet I couldn't believe this nightmare had become my reality. My husband's death devastated me. Life wasn't supposed to happen this way. We were meant to grow old together, raise our children together, and run our inn together. I was not supposed to be a widow or a single parent.

I thought I had finished grieving. Steve had battled metastatic melanoma for more than six years, and anticipatory grief had convinced me I was "ready" to move forward. I had cried all the tears. I had imagined the worst. I thought I'd done the work. But grief doesn't follow a schedule. It doesn't let you check a box early or skip the hard work.

When his death finally came, I tried to move forward. I kept busy raising two daughters, managing the inn, taking care of my parents, and volunteering in the community. I said yes to everyone and everything—except to my grief and to myself. I organized inn tours, attended committee meetings, and handled collections for the chamber of commerce. Too busy to think or feel. There was no time for the grief I thought I had dealt with. And that was okay with me.

I wasn't prepared for what was to come. I put one foot in front of the other and switched into autopilot. For the next five years, that was how I lived. I spent hours folding towels and sheets for the inn late into the night, sometimes past 11:00 p.m. I became the fitted sheet queen, folding them faster and better than anyone else. At 6:30 a.m., I started cooking breakfast. By 10:00 a.m., when breakfast service ended, I couldn't even remember what had been served.

Then it hit me. I had no choice but to acknowledge my grief and feel it. I cried at everything—TV commercials, books, movies, conversations. Coffee ads at Christmas and pleas to save animals brought me to my knees, sobbing uncontrollably. I truly let myself grieve. It was a whole new grief. The kind that sucker punches you at 2:00 a.m. The kind that leaves you wondering who you are without the one you lost.

Something shifted when I realized the life I was living wasn't mine. There was no Amy in it. So, I burned it down and began building a life where I was present in my family's life, the inn's life, and my own life.

Working with a coach cracked something open in me. I realized I had spent years suppressing ambition and assertiveness to make Steve seem stronger. I knew how to survive: pay bills, smile through pain, be everything for everyone. But I didn't know how to respect myself enough to stop. I had done everything I was told would make me happy, yet I felt like I was dying inside. I wasn't present in my life.

When I looked around the inn, almost everything was exactly the way it had been before Steve's death. Breakfast and afternoon refreshments followed his recipes. So, I introduced some new dishes and individual guest options when we weren't full. Cooking was never my favorite activity, but I felt proud to turn part of innkeeping into something that reflected me.

Business completely turned upside down when COVID-19 hit. At the beginning, we couldn't operate fully, then we were able to partially open without dining room service. I purchased equipment and provided room service, offering a rate for guests who opted out of food. As time moved on, we provided lunch and dinner options for guests who didn't want to go to restaurants—a risky, creative solution Steve might not have approved.

I also made a selective reduction in staff. Some employees didn't share my vision. In the past, I had no trouble letting go of employees who underperformed or didn't fit in. At the inn, it was different. We were more like a family than a business, working together almost daily for years. Since I lived and worked at the inn, there was minimal separation between my staff and me. It was like a fishbowl—we all knew each other's business, which made letting people go even harder. Although difficult, it was the right decision. Those who remained, or were hired later, shared my vision of hospitality and service.

Every change was scary. I wasn't sleeping well. I asked my mother and friends for advice but quickly realized it was all on me. Even though I had previously managed hospital departments and an in-home care agency, this was different. The buck stopped with me. I second-guessed every decision.

The quality of our linen service had dropped, so I ordered new towels, sheets, napkins, and tablecloths. It may seem trivial, but with twenty guest rooms and bathrooms, the number of each piece was huge—three linen sets per bed, four sets of towels for each night, thousands of dollars.

The marketing at the inn had also remained the same. I had

loved leading group programs in my previous life—so where were the groups here? I began by thinking about what I loved in my life and searching for groups I identified with: women's groups, spiritual groups, weekend programs for widows and widowers, programs for adoptive parents, business retreats, family retreats, and weddings.

I became a justice of the peace in Massachusetts and began performing weddings. The timing was perfect—Massachusetts had just legalized same-sex weddings. Believing in love, I saw this as a way to contribute to something meaningful. I remember one wedding on the front porch of the inn: two grooms who had been together for thirty years, finally united in marriage. Their love and excitement were palpable. A friend of theirs sang, one groom's daughter spoke, and they exchanged beautiful vows. Being around such love helped as I struggled to rebuild after my loss.

I hosted a women's retreat experiencing shamanic journeying without mind-altering substances. I was terrified of the idea of "traveling" and worried I might never return to my life. During the first ten attempts, all I did was fall asleep. It took a year before I could let go enough to journey. Then it happened: a small, Disney-like character came to me, took my hand, and led me through a magical forest where all the animals talked. I began to find answers to my questions and identify my direction.

Years later, during a journey, I saw myself sitting in a square in Mexico. It was colorful and loud, with music streaming from everywhere. I saw myself living there. I remember sharing that it was a great dream, but it would never happen. I owned the inn, was happy there, and had two grandchildren I wanted to spend time with. Two weeks later, a realtor approached me with a client interested in purchasing my inn. Even though I loved my life, I knew in my soul that the time was right for a change. Within three months, I sold and moved. The following spring, I found myself sitting in that very square in Mexico.

I pushed myself beyond my comfort zone and fear, sharing

myself with others. This became one of the greatest growth points to emerge from the ashes of my previous life—learning to get comfortable with being uncomfortable and allowing myself to be vulnerable. Making my own decisions with conviction and ease has become my new way of living.

I may have lost my husband and partner, but I gained something far more powerful: my voice, integrity, happiness, and freedom. I no longer hide behind anyone. I do not shrink. The ashes of my old life didn't bury me; they gave me the ground to rise from. The life I thought I had lost was never truly mine. What I built from the ashes is Amy, all the way.

Reflection

1. Where in your own life have you been living on autopilot, and what truths emerge when you finally pause to feel what you've been avoiding?

2. What part of yourself—your voice, your identity, your dreams—has been waiting quietly for permission to rise from the ashes?

3. What bold or unexpected step might help you move from merely surviving to fully living on your own terms?

What My Tumor Told Me

SARAH HAAS

As I watched the clear liquid, both poison and healing elixir, drip down the tube at a maddeningly slow pace, I tried not to dread what was to come. By round six of twenty, I was accustomed to the routine: treatment, exhaustion, nausea, slight recovery, repeat. Each treatment more brutal than the last, as my body became more and more depleted. I was terrified, anxious, and struggling to stay optimistic.

At forty-seven and in peak physical condition, I never imagined this would be me. A fitness trainer, distance runner, and yoga instructor, I was doing all the right things: eating healthy, meditating, and exercising. Yet here I was, bald, pale, and exhausted, with two angry red scars across my concave chest where my breasts had been. A shell of my old self.

Cancer doesn't discriminate.

When I received the diagnosis, two thoughts immediately went through my mind: "What if my children lose their mom?" and "Thank God I have an excuse to rest."

How could something as terrifying as a cancer diagnosis also carry a hint of relief?

I'd heard about celebrities being sent to a facility for "exhaustion" and had always thought how wonderful it would be to be relieved of all responsibilities and able to focus solely on rest and well-being.

Fear, grief, and shame crashed down on me like a ton of bricks.

For the next two years, my life was a flurry of tests, doctors, treatments, and surgeries. Always needles, always machines beeping, and always attached to tubes. The smell of antiseptic and the sight of other patients in various stages of the disease causing just as much nausea as the treatments themselves.

The physical side of cancer is brutal, but the mental and emotional work is ten times harder. I've always believed everything happens for a reason, and this journey was a true test of that belief.

To my surprise, the chemotherapy caused my eyesight to be so blurry I couldn't read, and my exhaustion, brain fog, pain, and nausea left me unable to focus or absorb information. I realized I was attempting to use my "rest time" to achieve and accomplish—exactly how I'd been living my life to this point.

My old habits and mindset had not yet shifted. I asked my higher power, the Universe of all-knowing energy, "What am I here to learn?"

The answer came loud and clear: "You don't need to *do* anything. Your work is just to *be*."

I realized I'd been hearing whispers from the Universe, and my own body, for years, telling me to slow down. The whispers grew louder and louder until I was hit over the head with this virtual sledgehammer. My body was forcing me to rest, slow down, release control, and let go of all I thought I "should" do.

My whole life I'd never felt I was *enough*. My career wasn't where it "should" be, my to-do list never caught up, and my house never clean. I was constantly tired but wired, seeing a counselor, taking medication for depression and anxiety, and drinking wine and watching television to quiet my mind.

Two voices were constantly pulling me in opposite directions. Do less. Do more. Slow down. Go faster.

Where had those voices come from?

Growing up, my family was extremely poor, sometimes without a car or even running water. My parents scrounging for quarters from my piggy bank just to do laundry.

I desperately wanted to fit in, but was so afraid of being rejected, I had very few close friendships and felt lonely and isolated.

I wanted so much to be accepted, so I focused on being as perfect as possible in two areas: academics and physical appearance. Always look pretty, do everything with a smile, be gracious, achieve, accomplish, keep moving, and, under no circumstances, ever, ever fail.

I created an outward identity. The perfect version of me that became an armor I wore to make people like me.

Schoolwork came easily to me, and I was naturally thin and athletic, but no matter what I achieved or how I looked, it was never good enough. The bar I set for myself was continuously raised.

My nose was too big, my teeth too crooked, and my grades never high enough. *Seventeen* magazine was both an obsession and a constant reminder that, in comparison, I could never measure up.

What I knew about myself intellectually, and how I felt about myself were always in contradiction. My head and my heart could never agree.

I was now struggling with the loss of the identity I'd worked so hard to create. I couldn't work, exercise, cook, or keep up with daily tasks. I couldn't be the mom I wanted to be for my kids. My hair was gone, my breasts were gone, my muscles were wasting. I no longer looked or felt like myself. It felt like punishment for vanity.

And yet, I received such an outpouring of love and support—home-cooked meals, gifts, cards, rides, and visits—not only from my family and close friends, but from past clients, acquaintances, and people I hadn't seen since high school.

Clearly, all those things I'd held onto so tightly were not why I was loved and accepted. My worth didn't come from my accomplishments or my physical appearance.

The next lesson was releasing the need to control. It's one of the hardest things I've ever done. I had no control over my own body or how I'd feel from day-to-day. I had no idea how I'd respond to the treatments, nor what the eventual outcome would be. I was constantly having to be vulnerable and open myself to invasive procedures when all I wanted to do was curl up and protect myself. All I could do was breathe, surrender to the process, and take each day and each step as it came.

This experience made me realize I'd been going through life with tunnel vision. Always so focused on controlling outcomes, I'd missed the whispers from the Divine along the way. When I released the need to control, I realized I could just *receive*. I didn't have to hold on tight, force, or work hard to be loved.

Healing my soul began with small acts of kindness to my body. Nourishing myself with fresh food, incorporating gentle movement, taking warm baths, and getting plenty of rest. I began to reconnect with my body and realize how strong, incredible, and resilient it is.

All this time I'd criticized, punished, and focused on my perceived flaws, while my body was doing everything I asked of it. My legs took me wherever I wanted to go. My arms and hands allowed me to work and do everything I needed to do. My stomach carried my children. My breasts fed them. My lungs breathed. My heartbeat. And now, my body was healing itself, recovering, and rebuilding.

My body is the most miraculous thing ever created. Gratitude for all I'd once criticized overflowed. Now I see the beauty in my scars, wrinkles, and stretch marks. They're my warrior wounds … proof of all I've been through and all I've overcome. Now, when my body talks, I listen.

Before I say *yes* to something, I pause and ask myself: "Am I doing this because I want to, or because I think I should?" "Am I doing this because I think I need to prove something or change someone's perception of me?" "If I say yes to this, am I saying no to myself?" "Is this in alignment with what truly matters and the vision I have for my life?"

What I know is important: relationships, time with those I love, and enjoying the present moment. What doesn't matter: looking perfect on the outside or molding myself to please others.

Sarah 2.0 is no longer stuck being small or preoccupied with trying to be perfect or looking like she "has it all." She accepts all the pieces of herself and embraces the imperfections that make her who she is. She takes up space. She shows up boldly and unapologetically. She's finally permitted herself to be authentically herself.

I'm always a work in progress. The old me still pipes up from time to time, but I know when that happens, it's just something within me asking to be seen, asking to be healed. My soul is whispering for attention. When I release the need to control and step into the flow, I can allow my angels to guide me.

I have a feather tattoo on my wrist, where I can see it every day, to remind me that angels are watching over me and that, no matter what happens, I am loved and protected.

I'm filled with peace and gratitude to be alive. To breathe. To be surrounded by love. And for the gift of this perfectly imperfect, beautiful life.

Reflection

1. If you could speak to the child you once were, what would you tell her?

2. What would you ten years from now, tell yourself in the present?

3. Which difficult situations in your life can you now look back on and realize were a gift?

Editor's Note

DEBORAH KEVIN, MA

When I first said yes to guiding *Embers to Wings*, I thought I understood what I was stepping into. After all, I've stewarded more anthologies into the world than I can count without taking off my shoes. But this book had other plans for me.

It didn't crash into my life with grand fanfare. It arrived softly—like the smallest ember—and then promptly set something inside me ablaze.

Each story you'll read has its own temperature. Some smolder. Some scorch. Some warm the palms like a mug of something comforting on a cold morning. And woven through every single one is a pulse of truth so potent, I often had to stop mid-edit just to breathe it in.

Then came the reflection questions.

I used to think of reflection questions as tidy little companions—gentle prompts to help readers sink deeper into meaning. But these? These were not tidy. These were doorways.

To write them, I had to slip back inside each woman's moment—into her disorientation, her courage, her unraveling, her rise—and listen for what her story was truly asking. What was trying to be illuminated? Invited? Released? Claimed?

Somewhere along the way, the questions started asking me things too.

Reflection, it turns out, is not a one-way street. It's a mirror with a generous sense of timing. More than once, I'd close my laptop feeling both cracked open and stitched together. Old wounds resurfaced, waving their hands like overeager 80s movie extras: "Hey! Remember us?" Tenderness expanded in my chest like a slow sunrise. And always, always, there was the unmistakable sense that transformation is contagious.

Because when you sit with another woman's truth long enough, your own truth starts clearing its throat.

Ask someone, *Where have you dimmed your light?*—and your own dimming rises to the surface. Ask, *What story are you ready to rewrite?*—and suddenly your own narrative is tapping its foot. Ask, *Where is your soul nudging you to say yes?*—and your yes becomes impossible to ignore.

Creating this anthology didn't just deepen the work. It deepened me. It held up a lantern to corners of my spirit I hadn't visited in far too long. The women in these pages didn't only offer their transformations—they made space for mine.

And now the invitation passes to you.

If you let them, these stories will settle into you. They will glow. They will widen what was too narrow and soften what was too tight. And the questions? Well … they might just open doors you didn't even realize were waiting.

Reading, like writing, can be a spiritual practice. A remembrance. A returning. A rising.

To every woman who entrusted us with her journey: thank you.

To every reader who will carry these sparks into her own life: I'm honored to walk beside you.

And to those barely there whispers within us all—the ones that shimmer at the edges of our awareness—may we keep listening. May we keep asking. And may we continue to rise, again and again.

About Our Authors

SHA BLACKBURN

Sha Blackburn, an internationally recognized psychic, intuitive confidence mentor, and teacher, known as The LoonWitch, has been empowering individuals to transform their lives using magickal principles and her intuitive gifts since 1997. Her teachings are based on the spiritual belief that "Everything Is Possible" and she leads coaching circles to remind women of the magick within. She is a Reiki master teacher, certified neuro-linguistic practitioner, QHHT practitioner, and a certified shamanic healer from the Foundation for Shamanic Studies. Learn more at http://www.loonwitch.com

SANDY COMBS

Sandy Combs is a Soul Guide and self-proclaimed "Joyologist." Surviving two near-death experiences by age six, Sandy's psychic gifts were fully awakened. Deeply communicating with Spirit enabled Sandy to walk her way out of trauma and embrace a life of wholeness. Sandy's greatest mission in life is helping others develop their intuitive gifts and find wholeness using elemental wisdom, astrology, energy medicine, and creativity. Learn more at http://www.sandy-combs.com.

RINAT DE PICCIOTTO

Rinat De Picciotto is a transformational coach and brand designer who helps women shed limiting identities and step into the fullness of their being. Whether guiding purpose discovery or supporting entrepreneurs to create aligned brands, she merges Feminine Power coaching with design that reflects their soul's blueprint. Her work awakens clarity, confidence, and authentic expression—empowering women to embody their essence, step into their power, and create with purpose and impact. Learn more at https://www.rinatdepicciotto.ca.

ANDRA EVANS

Andra Evans is a professional spiritual director and companion, guiding women through the inner spiritual terrains during the midlife initiation and menopausal journey. This is a heroine's journey, where Andra walks with women to discover next-level inner power through the call to heal and to take the next empowered steps in life. Find a free "soul map" of this journey at her website below, along with soul support at her blog, *Andorra's Box*. Learn more at http://www.soulexpressions.ca.

ENGRACIA GILL

Engracia Gill lives in Austin, Texas. She loves working in private practice and has done so for the last twenty-four years. She guides individuals through trusted body-mind techniques to free the body of the sequelae of trauma. She teaches mindfulness tools to transform pain. She deeply believes in the human psyche's ability to transcend emotional pain and suffering. Her deepest joy is to serve as a facilitator to her clients' healing journey. Connect with her at www.engraciagill.com.

KIM GORE

Kim Gore is a passionate advocate for and supporter of women's dreams. As a gifted *belief excavator*, she has the innate ability to ask deep questions that help women reframe and remodel out-dated patterns, creating a sound foundation so they can thrive in every chapter of their lives. She is passionate about empowering women with the tools and supportive containers to help them believe in themselves, their dreams, and the possibilities within. You can find her at www.u2canthrive.com.

KELLEY GRIMES

Kelley Grimes, MSW, is an empowering counselor, speaker, and workshop facilitator, self-nurturing expert, Aspire Magazine Expert Columnist, and best-selling author of *The Art of Self-Nurturing: A Field Guide to Living with More Peace, Joy, and Meaning*. She inspires individuals and organizations to nurture peace, compassion, and hope in the world from the inside out. Kelley lives in Carlsbad, California, in a four-generational household, is married to an artist and board game maker, and loves traveling, painting, singing, and playing with her adorable grandchildren. Learn more at www.cultivatingpeaceandjoy.com.

JORDAN GUADALUPE

Jordan Guadalupe has spent nearly two decades studying the law of attraction and the art of self-mastery. As a manifestation coach, she helps entrepreneurs and professionals break free from playing small and instead step into success, wealth, and joy through her signature mindset-transformation approach. Her clients dissolve self-sabotaging patterns and create lives grounded in fulfillment, freedom, and soul-aligned possibility. Rooted in spirituality, Jordan's work reflects how she lives—present, intuitive, and always dreaming up her next global adventure. When she's not coaching, you'll likely find her paddleboarding or soaking in the beauty of the moment. Learn more at www.soulibre.life.

SARAH HAAS

Sarah Haas is a women's weight-loss and body-love coach, Integrative Nutrition Health coach, certified personal trainer, yoga instructor, host of the *Boss Body* podcast, and expert columnist for *Aspire Magazine*. She supports women in midlife, menopause, and beyond to create vibrant health, feel good in their bodies, and live a simple, sustainable, healthy lifestyle. Her holistic approach weaves together nutrition, body movement, self-compassion, and radical self-love. You can learn more about Sarah and her work at http://www.sarahhaaswellness.com.

SHARIE HOHN

Sharie Hohn is the founder of Illuminate Your Potentials and a Guide to Living Your Light. With over thirty years of experience as a clinician, natural health educator, and energy healer, she empowers women to release old patterns, rebuild self-worth, and embody authentic joy. Through holistic practices that align body, mind, and spirit, Sharie guides women in reconnecting with their health, soul truth, and full potential to create lives of freedom and possibility. Connect with her at www.shariehohn.com.

LISA HROMADA

Lisa Hromada is a spiritual life coach, author, and international best-selling coauthor. After experiencing a Divine Reset™, she created the Empowered Lifeview™ methodology to help women overcome challenges, reclaim peace, and live with clarity and spiritual connection. Through her free Divine Reset™ and Empowered Lifeview™ gift sets and self-paced course, *The Divine Reset™ Experience*, Lisa offers soul-aligned meditations and mindset recalibration tools for fast, transformational results. Learn more at www.loveistheseed.com.

YVETTE LEFLORE

Yvette LeFlore is a Reiki Master teacher and intuitive energy healer based in Virginia. She has guided hundreds of clients and students in discovering the power of energy healing to support transformation, balance, and self-discovery. Through her teaching and healing practice, Yvette creates safe, soulful spaces for people to reconnect with themselves, release what no longer serves them, and step into new possibilities. Visit www.healingwithyvette.com to learn more.

RUTHIE LEWIS

Ruthie Lewis is a soul-wellness and mindset coach, author, and retreat leader. Through a long, arduous journey of self-doubt and sacrifice, her passion became guiding women from restrictive, programmed beliefs of "have-tos" and "supposed-tos" to Let Your Glow Show. She invites overwhelmed women to make the courageous decision to discover that the secret to life is the awakening and freeing of what has been asleep. Ruthie is available to speak and offers many coaching opportunities. Connect with Ruthie at www.ruthielewis.com.

AMY LINDNER-LESSER

Amy Lindner-Lesser, MS.W., is a three-time best-selling author, podcaster, speaker, and certified grief and life transitions coach with over four decades of experience. She's supported hundreds of individuals through life's transitions as a coach, mentor, and guide, helping them turn painful chapters into meaningful, soulled lives where mere survival is replaced by joy and thriving. Learn more at www.inntrospection.com.

REV. FELICIA MESSINA-D'HAITI

Rev. Felicia Messina-D'Haiti lovingly supports others in clearing physical, mental, emotional, and spiritual blockages to bring greater alignment to their homes and lives. Felicia is a Feng Shui and Soul Coaching® Trainer and Practitioner, passionate about empowering others through teaching. She is a speaker, award-winning educator, and contributing author or several best-selling books. Connect with Felicia at www.feliciadhaiti.com, receive a complimentary gift, and explore her offerings, including certification courses in feng shui, clutter clearing, space clearing, Soul Coaching®, and Usui Reiki.

BETH MYERS

Beth Myers is a natural-born soul guide who walks beside women on their journey of transformation. Drawing on decades of experience as an educator, school counselor, and coach, she empowers women to release limiting stories, reclaim their inner light, and rediscover the joy within. Merging her compassionate guidance and energy mastery tools, Beth supports women in remembering their REAL™ truth (Real Empowerment Allows Love™), co-creating their next chapter, and rising with confidence. Learn more at www.u2canthrive.com.

NANCY OKEEFE

Nancy OKeefe is a certified Human Design business coach who guides women entrepreneurs to make a bigger difference by leveraging their Human Design to stand out as experts, create distinction, fuel demand for their services, and lead their niche to grow a successful and fulfilling business. Nancy is a bestselling author, an expert columnist for *Aspire Magazine*, a certified executive coach, and holds an MBA from Babson College in Entrepreneurship. Learn more at www.nancyokeefecoaching.com.

JESSICA BANE ROBERT

Jessica Bane Robert, is a professor of mindfulness at Clark University and the founder of the Barred Owl Retreat Center in Leicester, Massachusetts. With over twenty years of experience, Jessica has honed her gifts to become a transformational mindfulness coach, sound healer, forest bathing guide, NLP coach, writer, and speaker. Her nurturing workshops and retreats focus on holistic mindfulness-based practices, creative expression, and nature connection. She supports women in navigating the unknown, reconnecting with their inner wisdom, and creating lives fueled by clarity, purpose, and peace. Learn more at www.barredowlretreat.com.

KELLYANN (KELLY) SCHAEFER

Kellyann (Kelly) Schaefer is an entrepreneur, mentor, and author who helps others grow purpose-driven service businesses through her company, The Concierge Academy. Drawing from years of real-world experience, she teaches practical, sustainable ways to build success while creating more freedom and impact. Beyond business, Kelly is passionate about growth, community, and living life fully and showing others that success is most powerful when it's built from a place of authenticity and heart. Learn more by visiting www.theconciergeacademy.com.

APRIL SMALL

April Small, master life coach and therapeutic art life coach, is dedicated to blending her psychology background with her artistic training to help others embrace their creative heART. She invites her clients to trust what flows through them and to discover creativity as a powerful pathway to self-care and self-discovery. Learn more at www.odonataartisticservices.com.

JENNIFER "JENNIFIRE" SULLIVAN

Jennifer "Jennifire" Sullivan is a transformational spiritual mentor and animal communicator with over two decades of experience in astrology, tarot, and the intuitive arts. A certified master fire walk facilitator, she blends ancient wisdom with practical techniques to spark life-changing breakthroughs. Jennifer supports spiritual journeys through personalized readings, sound healings, retreats, and ceremonial events. Her own journey has helped her create a results-driven, heart-centered approach that enables clients to release limiting beliefs, embody authenticity, and stride confidently toward healing, harmony, and freedom. Learn more at www.jennifer-sullivan.com.

ELAINE C. TORRANCE-GINGRICH

Elaine C. Torrance-Gingrich is an ordained minister, certified coach, clinical hypnotherapist, certified conscious dance facilitator, certified Groove and Groove FIT facilitator, and law of attraction practitioner. Known as the goddess of pleasure and possibilities, her passion is to help women heal, align, and rise into their feminine power by guiding them into sacred wealth, energetic embodiment, and emotional remembrance so they can create soul-aligned lives and businesses rooted in pleasure and possibility. Learn more at www.avalonianmoon.com.

JANNA LYNN WELLEMEYER

Janna Lynn Wellemeyer knows that healing is not linear. Drawing on modalities such as The Grief Recovery Method, Shamanic teachings, and Reiki, she has walked her own path toward meaning and joy—work that now fuels her passion for supporting others. With compassion and a safe, steady presence, she helps clients address unresolved trauma and invite more peace and joy into their lives. She would be honored to walk beside you on your journey. Learn more at www.jannawellemeyer.com.

LEE MURPHY WOLF

Lee Murphy Wolf, Expansion Catalyst™ and evolutionary guide, mentors soul-led women who feel called to a higher, more aligned purpose. She supports them in releasing the energetic patterns that keep them small, reconnecting with their truest selves, and rediscovering their deepest desires. Her work empowers women to step into the visionary leadership they're meant to embody—both in life and in business. Learn more at www.leemurphywolf.com.

About Our Publisher

LINDA JOY

Founded in 2010 by Sacred Visibility™ Catalyst, Mindset Elevation Coach, and *Aspire Magazine* Publisher Linda Joy, Inspired Living Publishing, LLC (ILP) is a best-selling boutique hybrid publishing company.

Dedicated to publishing books for women and by women and to spreading a message of love, positivity, feminine wisdom, and self-empowerment to women of all ages, backgrounds, and life paths—Inspired Living Publishing's books have reached numerous international bestsellers lists as well as Amazon's Movers & Shakers lists.

Through Inspired Living Publishing's highly successful sacred anthology division, hundreds of visionary female entrepreneurs have written their sacred soul stories using ILP's Authentic Storytelling® writing model and become best-selling authors.

Linda also works privately with empowered women entrepreneurs and messengers through her Illuminate Sistermind™ group program and private coaching.

Linda's other inspirational brands include Inspired Living University™, Inspired Living Secrets™, Inspired Living Give-away™, and her popular radio show, *Inspired Conversations*.

Learn more about Linda's private work and offerings at www.Linda-Joy.com.

About Our Managing Editor

DEBORAH KEVIN

Deborah Kevin is the founder of Highlander Press, host of the *STORYTELLHER* podcast, best-selling author of *Shelf Life: A Field Guide to Long-Term Author Success*, and an unapologetic disruptor of the status quo. She's on a mission to elevate women's voices and help changemakers share their stories with impact and heart. An adventurer at heart, Debby has trekked the Camino de Santiago and thrives on exploring the world with her family. A magic believer, French Press enthusiast, and master of irreverent humor, she brings warmth, wit, and bold truth-telling to everything she touches.

About Our Associate Editor

LINDA DESSAU

Linda Dessau of LD Editorial has been exploring creativity for many years, from writing stories and singing in choirs to building a thriving music therapy practice. In 2005, she returned to her love for the written word and has since helped dozens of authors and business owners clarify and polish their writing. She is keenly attentive to the author's voice and to being a collaborative and supportive partner in the writing process.

About Our Associate Editor

CHELSEA SEEGMILLER

Chelsea Seegmiller is the owner of Ellipsis Editorial, an agency specializing in academic, scholarly, and literary editorial support. She works on projects ranging from legal reports and short stories to peer-reviewed journals and full-length novels. She is passionate about helping authors, publishers, and legal professionals enhance their writing through precise and thoughtful editing.

Inspired Living Publishing ~ Transforming Women's Lives, One Story at a Time™

If you enjoyed this book, visit
www.InspiredLivingPublishing.com

and sign up for ILP's e-zine to receive news about hot new releases,
promotions, and information on exciting author events.